ISLAMIC ARMS
AND ARMOUR

Thom Richardson

CONTENTS

Front cover: Helmet (*migfer*). XXVIA.142, 146

Page 1: Shield (*kalkan*). XXVIA.126

Page 2: Sword (*talwar*). AL.290 60 Royal Collection Trust/© Her Majesty Queen Elizabeth II 2015

Back cover: Snaphaunce sporting gun (*mukhala*). XXVIF.134

FOREWORD

The Royal Armouries collection of Asian arms and armour is among the finest in the world, and it has been my privilege to curate it for the last 25 years. The collection is unique in its broad coverage of every part of Asia, and in the early provenances that many of the pieces, especially those from the Indian subcontinent, have. Much of the collection was acquired before 1870, and important documentary information about the objects was recorded. By the late 19th century the collection was an important feature in the Tower Armouries' displays, but in the 20th century it underwent some vicissitudes, being passed wholesale to the British Museum in 1914 and returned in the 1970s. The practice of renumbering objects in the collection was followed by the Armouries more than most museums in the 19th century, and so re-establishing connection between the earliest records and the current objects was an important part of the documentation of the collection that occupied much of my work in the 1980s. The redisplay of the collection in the spacious Oriental Gallery in Leeds enabled it to be shown off to better advantage, and for many new acquisitions to be incorporated in the permanent display. The emphasis of the gallery and this series of books is on the geographical and temporal periods covered by the collection, and as very little of the Asian collection pre-dates 1400, and most of it belongs to the 17th to 19th century, that is the area to which emphasis has been given, though I have attempted to paint a brief picture of what had occurred before. The end point is the mass introduction of firearms from the West, and the relative homogenisation of what had been a rich and vibrant diversity of military cultures. The publication of this facet of the Asian collection follows on from my earlier *Introduction to Indian Arms and Armour*, and my colleague Ian Bottomley's *Introductions to Japanese Armour* and *Japanese Swords*.

I hope these publications will inspire a new interest in those who do not know about the objects, and provide some new published examples for those who do.

Thom Richardson
Deputy Master, Royal Armouries

INTRODUCTION

The expansion of Islam, both as a religion and as an imperial power, is one of the extraordinary dramas of world history. The Hegira (flight or migration) of the Prophet Muhammad and his forces from Mecca to Medina occurred in 622. Victory two years later at the battle of Badr (624) established Muhammad's ascendancy over the Hejaz in western Arabia, and by the time of his death in 632 his authority was supreme in most of Arabia.

Empire-building

Under the first four caliphs who succeeded Muhammad from 632–61 an empire was created which spread from Tripoli in the west to Tiflis in the north and to Herat and Merv in the east. Under the Umayyad caliphs (661–750) the empire was extended to incorporate the north African coast, Spain and parts of the south of France in the west, and in the east Afghanistan, Pakistan up to the River Indus,

▼ The Arabian Empire in AD 751.

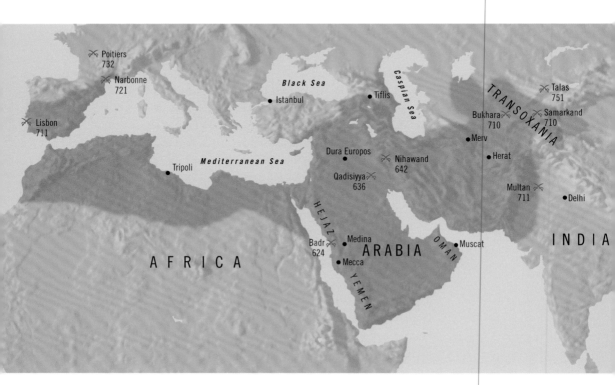

Turkmeniya, Uzbekistan and Tadzhikistan. The major towns at the extremities of the empire were taken in the early 8th century: Bukhara and Samarkand in 710, Multan in 711, Lisbon in the same year, Narbonne in 721. The forces of Islam were turned back in 732 by the Franks at the battle of Poitiers, and by the Turks at Talas in 751. The first great phase of Muslim expansion, an area spanning six time zones, took less than a century. A thousand years later, by the 17th century, the area of Islamic religious influence or political control stretched from Northwest Africa through the Middle East into Eastern Europe, across Central Asia, into the Indian sub-continent and across Southeast Asia as far as the Philippines.

Dating Islamic Objects

During the medieval and later period a number of different systems of dating were used in the Islamic world. The commonest was the Muslim *hijri* dating, which starts from the flight of the Prophet Muhammad from Mecca to Medina (the *Hegira*) on 15 July AD 622. This is a lunar calendar of 12 months, or 354/5 days, so gains a year on the Christian calendar every 33/4 years. A variation on the *hijri* dating, a solar calendar starting from the birth of the Prophet Muhammad in AD 571, called the Mauludi era, was introduced by Tipu Sultan of Mysore.

▶ Chiselled decoration on the barrel of a sporting gun made in Seringapatam for Tipu Sultan, dated 1794/5 (1223 AM), highlighted in the circle. XXVIF.46

▼ Numbers 0-9 in Arabic used in *hijri* dates.

0	1	2	3	4	5	6	7	8	9
٠	١	٢	٣	٤	٥	٦	٧	٨	٩

Sunni and Shi'a

Early in Islamic history a difference arose between two Muslim sects, the Sunni and Shi'a. The Sunni are so called because they accept the *Sunna* (a body of sayings ascribed to the prophet Muhammad) as of equal authority with the *Qur'an*, the holy book of Islam. The Shi'a ascribe divine status to 'Ali, the cousin and brother-in-law of Muhammad, and his successors, and await the coming of a *Mahdi* (messiah). The differences between the two sects are profound, extending to all aspects of life, both religious and secular. In particular the Imams (religious leaders) exert absolute authority under Shi'i Islam, whereas they only have the role of advisers under Sunni Islam.

The Sassanid Persian Empire

The main victim of Islamic expansion was the Sassanid Persian Empire. The Sassanids, in turn, had constructed their empire in a militant Iranian revolt in AD 224 against the Central Asian Parthians, who between 247 and 141 BC had ousted the Seleucid successors of Alexander the Great in their eastern Hellenistic empire. The forces of the Parthians used the characteristic Central Asian tactics: large forces of light horse archers supported by heavy cavalry wearing scale armour and riding barded horses, equipped with bows but also charging with the lance. Superbly preserved examples of their equipment have been excavated from Dura Europos on the Roman frontier, including horse armours and shields, while one of the few early composite bows was found nearby.

▲ Graffito of a Sassanid cataphract from Dura-Europos, 3rd century AD.

The Sassanids continued the Parthian military system, with changes in emphasis: armoured knights (*fursan*) became more important and numerous, and infantry (*rijjala*) became more significant too. In a 6th-century review of Khusrau Anushirvan's army (*jund*), 'Each knight was to have horse armour (*tajfaf*), mail armour (*dir'*), a lamellar coat (*jawshan*), leg defences (*saq*), a sword (*saif*), a lance (*rumh*), a shield (*turs*), either an axe (*tabarzin*) or a mace ('*amud*), a bowcase with two bows and their strings, thirty arrows and two extra bowstrings which the knight should attach to the rear of his helmet.'

Of the extensive Sassanian military kit, so reminiscent of Central Asian knights like the Khitan, only the helmets and swords survive in any quantities, together with one fragmentary *jawshan*. Sassanian equipment was adopted by the Arabian invaders, and further links with central Asian equipment were forged by the use of Khurasanian and later Turkish *ghulam* cavalry under the Abbasid caliphate (750–936).

Swords

The sword was of great symbolic importance under Islam, and the sword of the Prophet, 'Dhu'l Faqar', wielded by him at the battle of Badr, passed on to the caliph 'Ali; its blade, cloven in two at the point, has been used on banners ever since. An important group of early Islamic swords, including two associated with the Prophet himself, are preserved in the Topkapı Saray in Istanbul. All but one of these has a broad, straight, double-edged blade, and some have been fitted with later hilts during the 13th to 16th centuries. The dating of the original blades presents considerable problems, for such blades continued to be used until the 15th century, and continued in Islamic Africa as the precursors of the 19th-century *kaskara*.

Islamic Art and Decoration

Though Islam does not strictly forbid the representation of human figures, its art has tended to concentrate on geometrical and natural motifs, and above all calligraphy, especially of the words of the Prophet which formed the sacred book of Islam, the *Qur'an*. Thus much of the decoration of arms and armour across the Islamic world is calligraphic. Furthermore, the requirement to read the *Qur'an* in Arabic led to the use of Arabic script for most of the languages of the Islamic world. Thus Persian, Urdu, Pashto and Turkish (until the formation of the republic in 1923) and many others were or are still written in Arabic script. The importance of calligraphy and its profusion led to the developments of a number of different styles of writing, the most important of which are nashki, nasta'liq, thuluth and the angular kufic.

◀ Hilt detail of curved sword (*talwar*) and scabbard.
AL.290 60 Royal Collection Trust/© Her Majesty Queen Elizabeth II 2015

MEDIEVAL ISLAM

The armour styles imported into Islam from Sassanid Persia continued to be used until the time of the Mongol invasion in the 13th century. The remarkable Fatih Album preserved in the Topkapı Saray library in Istanbul illustrates the arms and armour of the later Mongol kingdoms in the west, and is an example of the way in which Chinese art was spread by the Mongols. In the 14th and 15th centuries a new style of armour appeared in the Islamic world.

◀▶ Cavalry and infantry from the 14th-century Fatih Album. This remarkable album illustrates the forces of the later Mongol kingdoms in the west, and is an example of the way in which Chinese art was spread by the Mongols.

Topkapı Saray Library, Istanbul H.2153, fos. 3b-4a, 87a (detail)

In Europe technological developments, probably the creation of more powerful crossbows spanned by mechanical devices, led to the addition of solid plate armour worn over the top of defences of mail. In the Islamic world, plate defences were made as part of the mail garments, and the lamellar coats which had been worn over the top of mail ceased to be used. These mail and plate defences, called *jawshan*, had numerous columns of overlapping plates at the front and rear, all joined together and articulated by rows of mail. From the later 15th century very large numbers of these coats, as well as the helmets and other pieces of armour that were worn with them, survive. The characteristic conical helmets of the Islamic world also owe their origins to the Sassanid military tradition. Almost all the surviving examples come from a single source, the old Byzantine Church of the Sacred Peace, Haghia Irene, in Istanbul, which was set up as a monument to the victories of the Ottoman Turks, and forms the collections of medieval arms and armour which can be seen in the Topkapı Saray and Askeri Museums in Istanbul today. One distinctive form, known as the 'turban' helmet, whose skull shares the same onion shape as the dome of a mosque, is particularly characteristic of the Islamic world.

▲ Battle scene from the Demotte Shahnameh 1340–50. Detroit Institute of Arts

▶ Battle scene from a Shahnameh 1370–80. Topkapı Saray Library, Istanbul H.762, fo. 51a

◀ **Bronze Mace Head**
Iranian, 12th century. Purchased 2000. XXVIC.77

The Timurid dynasty (1370–1506) was the last great Mongol 'successor kingdom' to rule Persia. It was founded by Timur (known in the West as Tamurlane), whose family claimed descent from Genghis Khan and ruled from Samarkand. Between 1395 and 1402, from his base in Transoxania, Timur's armies engaged in ferocious campaigns west through Persia to Anatolia, east into India as far as Delhi and north to Moscow. He died before the start of a planned expedition into China. Timur's armies were traditional steppe cavalry forces. Mail and plate armour for man and horse became the standard type of equipment for the heavy cavalry under the Timurids. These cavalry, armed with bow, sword and sometimes lance, were the main component of all the medieval Islamic armies. Horse armour was very important in most of the medieval Muslim kingdoms, for the bow was the most important weapon on the battlefield, and horses were vulnerable to archery. Other kingdoms not conquered by the Mongols included the Qara Qoyonlu or 'Black Sheep' who occupied Azerbaijan and Iraq from 1380 to 1468. They were conquered by the ak-Koyonlu or 'White Sheep' Turks of eastern Anatolia. These in turn were defeated by the Ottomans and were absorbed by Persia's Safavid dynasty in the early 1500s.

◄ The cavalry of the Timurids in action, from the 14th-century Fatih Album.

Topkapı Saray Library, Istanbul H.2153, fo. 102a

GUNPOWDER WEAPONS

▲ Ceramic grenade

Possibly Syrian, 13th century.
Transferred from the Royal
United Services Institute, 1962.
XXVIM.9

Before the spread of gunpowder technology from China to the West, other forms of incendiaries were used in warfare. In the Byzantine world 'Greek fire' was used, either sprayed from 'flame-throwers' on board ships or in the form of hand or machine-hurled pots of explosive or grenades. The constituents were kept secret, and scholars have speculated on its composition, as to whether it was a form of gunpowder (a mixture of sulphur, saltpetre and carbon), or a compound based on quicklime, or one based on petroleum products, such as naptha (Arabic *naft*). The ceramic grenades became popular among the Islamic kingdoms, and a factory for their manufacture has been excavated at Hama in Syria.

▲ Hand cannon

Mamluk Egypt or Syria,
1497–8. Purchased 2013.
XXVIF.245

This bronze hand cannon has a short, wide barrel and a long, narrow breech. It is inscribed 'mimma 'umila bi-rasm al-maqarr/al-ali, Kertbey al-Ahmar', made to order of his highness Kertbey al-Ahmar (Mamluk governor of Damascus 1497–8). It was originally fitted with a long wooden tiller, attached to an iron tang which protruded from the breech.

HELMETS

The 'turban' helmet or *migfer* went out of fashion early in the 16th century, to be replaced by the *çiçak*, an open-faced helmet with plate cheekpieces and neckguard. It prompted the same development in European helmets in the 17th century.

▶ Helmet (*migfer*)

Turkish, ak-Koyonlu, late 15th century. Purchased 1843; from the arsenal of Haghia Irene, Istanbul. XXVIA.142, 146

Arabic calligraphy was used as decoration on very many Islamic pieces. The inscriptions in gold and silver on this particularly fine ak-Koyonlu helmet of the late 15th century. Around the upper part is a stanza from a popular poem of the 15th century: *li-sahibini al-sa'ada wa'l-salam wa'l-afiya wa tul al-amara sazahat hamana (to its owner good fortune, peace, and health throughout his lifetime as long as the doves coo).*

The lower band is a series of titles of an unnamed sultan, most probably Y'aqub ibn Uzun Hasan (r. 1478–90): *Al-mu'izz al-mawid-malik al-mansur 'izza al-'izz wa'l-iqbal wa'l-dawla wa'l-sultan wa'l-salam wa'l-'afiya wa'l-dawla (Glorifier of the faith, victorious, triumphant king, to him be lasting glory, prosperity, power, peace, health and wealth).*

◀ Turban helmet (*migfer*)

Persian, Timurid, late 15th century. Purchased 1842; from the arsenal of Haghia Irene, Istanbul. XXVIA.125

The helmets used by the Mongolian successor kingdom of Timur (Tamurlane) were similar to those of the Ottoman and ak-Koyonlu Turks. They are distinguished by the use of the angular Kufic script for their inscriptions.

Dismounted *sipahi* from Melchior Lorck's series of prints featuring Turkish costume published in Augsburg in 1626. I.959

▶ Helmet (*çiçak*)

Turkish, early 16th century. Purchased 1842; from the arsenal of Haghia Irene, Istanbul. XXVIA.147

This is the transitional form between the 'turban' helmet and the çiçak – a helmet with a peak and a long mail aventail. It has been much repaired during its working life, and its aventail has been extended.

ARMOUR

▶ Brigandine (*karkal*)

Turkish, probably
15th century. XXVIA.263

Brigandine is the
European term for a
defence composed of
iron plates riveted inside
a fabric coat. Islamic
examples of these
defences are rare.

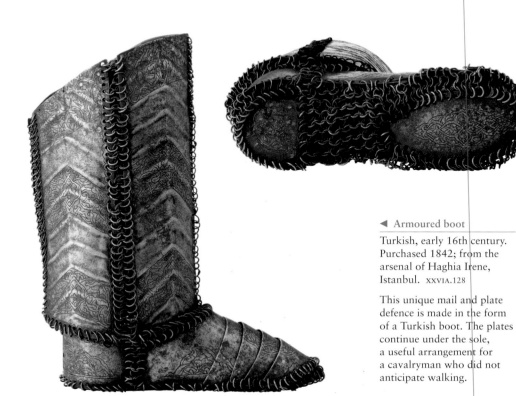

◀ Armoured boot

Turkish, early 16th century.
Purchased 1842; from the
arsenal of Haghia Irene,
Istanbul. XXVIA.128

This unique mail and plate
defence is made in the form
of a Turkish boot. The plates
continue under the sole,
a useful arrangement for
a cavalryman who did not
anticipate walking.

Turkish, late 15th century. Purchased 1842; from the arsenal of Haghia Irene, Istanbul. XXVIA.245

This coat has had a long working life. The plates come from a number of different coats, as is shown by the different types of decoration. Armour was always a valuable commodity, and was re-used as long as possible.

▶ Mail hood and shirt (*zirh*)

Probably Persian, late 15th century. Purchased 1974. XXVIA.145, 270

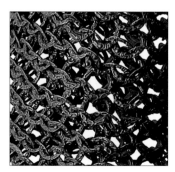

Detail of the mail showing the inscriptions on the riveted links.

HORSE ARMOUR

Shaffron (*at alinlici*)

Turkish, ak-Koyonlu, late 15th century. Purchased 1842; from the arsenal of Haghia Irene, Istanbul. xxvIH.3

This is one of the finest Turkish shaffrons of the period. The decoration includes several inscriptions, giving the titles but not the name of the Sultan (probably the ak-Koyonlu Ya'qub ibn Uzun Hasan, r. 1478–90) under whom its owner served: *'everlasting glory, prosperity, wealth and good fortune'* and *'oh! Greatest sultan, most exalted emperor, the master who curbs nations, of the kings of the Arabs and non-Arabs'*.

Detail of the dragon and inscription on the boss.

◀ Battle scene about 1493.

C13602-91 Add.25900, f231v
© The British Library Board

HAMMERS

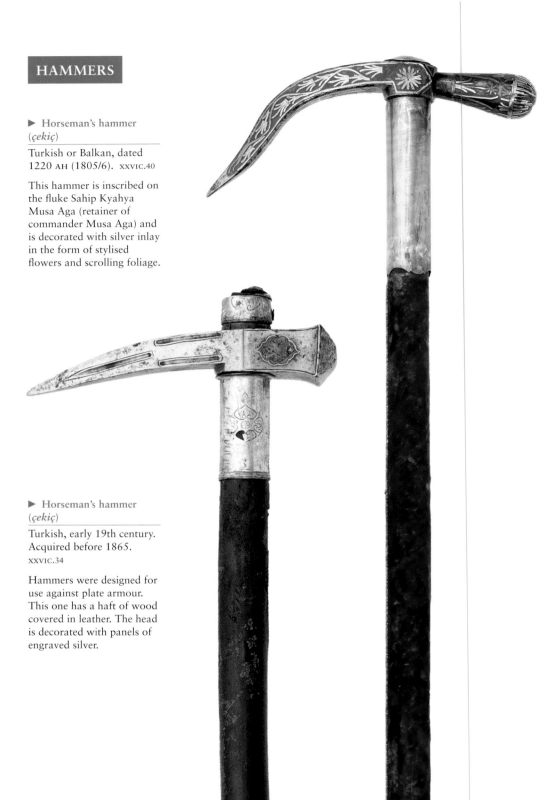

► Horseman's hammer
(*çekiç*)

Turkish or Balkan, dated
1220 AH (1805/6). XXVIC.40

This hammer is inscribed on
the fluke Sahip Kyahya
Musa Aga (retainer of
commander Musa Aga) and
is decorated with silver inlay
in the form of stylised
flowers and scrolling foliage.

► Horseman's hammer
(*çekiç*)

Turkish, early 19th century.
Acquired before 1865.
XXVIC.34

Hammers were designed for
use against plate armour.
This one has a haft of wood
covered in leather. The head
is decorated with panels of
engraved silver.

SHIELDS

◄ Shield (*separ*)

Probably Turkish, ak-Koyonlu, late 15th century. Purchased 1842; from the arsenal of Haghia Irene, Istanbul. XXVIA.127

The calligraphy on this shield records the titles of an unnamed ak-Koyonlu sultan, probably Ya'qub (1478–90). The central panel is earlier, and includes the name of the Timurid khan Ulugh Beg (1394–1449). Though it is made of steel it weighs less than the usual cane *kalkan* (1.71 kg, compared with 2.01 kg), and would have been used in battle as well as for parades.

Shield interior showing plaited leather handgrip and fragments of suspension strap.

◄ Shield (*kalkan*)

Turkish, 17th century. Acquired before 1859. XXVIA.126

This shield is formed of canes woven together with coloured silk to form a pattern. It is typical of the shields used by medieval Muslim cavalry all over Asia. Many of these shields were taken during the Ottoman assault on Vienna in 1683.

آل باش جراغنده طومدی هوا | لاجوردایکین سپیاه اولدی سما

شرق شناسی داخی اول کن صبحدم علم | حشمت ابله بندی قالدُردی سما

THE OTTOMAN TURKS

The battle of Çaldiran, 1514. Selimname.

Topkapı Saray Library, Istanbul H.1597-98, fo.113a

▼ The Ottoman Turkish Empire in 1600.

Turkish auxiliaries started to enter Muslim service in the 10th century. Between 1038 and 1071 the Oghuz Turks founded the Seljuq Empire, extending from Afghanistan in the east to Anatolia in the west. After the Mongol conquests of the 13th century a number of Turkish states re-asserted themselves, including the Seljuq Sultanate of Rum ('Rome', as it occupied some of the former Byzantine or Roman Empire). The Sultanate broke up in the early 14th century, and one of the successor Ghazi states under Osman I founded in western Anatolia a sultanate which grew into the mighty Ottoman Empire. In the 14th century they expanded into the Balkans, defeating the Serbs at Kosovo in 1389 and the Crusaders at Nicopolis in 1396. Constantinople was captured in 1453 and renamed Istanbul.

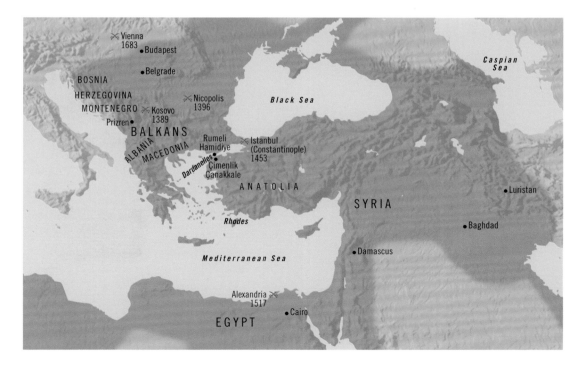

CAVALRY AND INFANTRY

The strength of these Turkish military forces derived from a combination of traditional steppe cavalry warfare, based on a combination of light and heavy cavalry, all bow armed, called *akinjis* and *sipahis* respectively, together with disciplined, effective infantry (the *janissaries*) and from their early use of firearms. Almost all of the surviving examples of medieval Islamic armour come from the Byzantine Church of the Sacred Peace, Haghia Irene, in Istanbul, which was converted into a monument to the victories of the Turks after the capture of Constantinople. The mark with which they are stamped is the *tamgha* of the Kayi tribe, one of the leading Oghuz tribes before the foundation of the Ottoman Empire. The armours from Haghia Irene in the Royal Armouries collection were bought in 1841 through the agency of Lord Curzon, via the notorious London dealer Samuel Luke Pratt. More of Pratt's purchases can be seen in the Tournament gallery in Leeds.

▲ Haghia Irene. Gryffindor

▲ The *tamgha* of the Kayi tribe.

◄ From a series of German 17th-century woodblock prints of Turks by Melchior Lorck. Cavalryman (*sipahi*) and Infantryman (*saq karabigitler*). I.959

▶ Funeral of Sultan Suleyman the Magnificent from the History of Sultan Suleyman, 1579 (AH 987), Istanbul, Turkey.

Detail showing mail and
plate construction.

Detail showing mail and
plate construction.

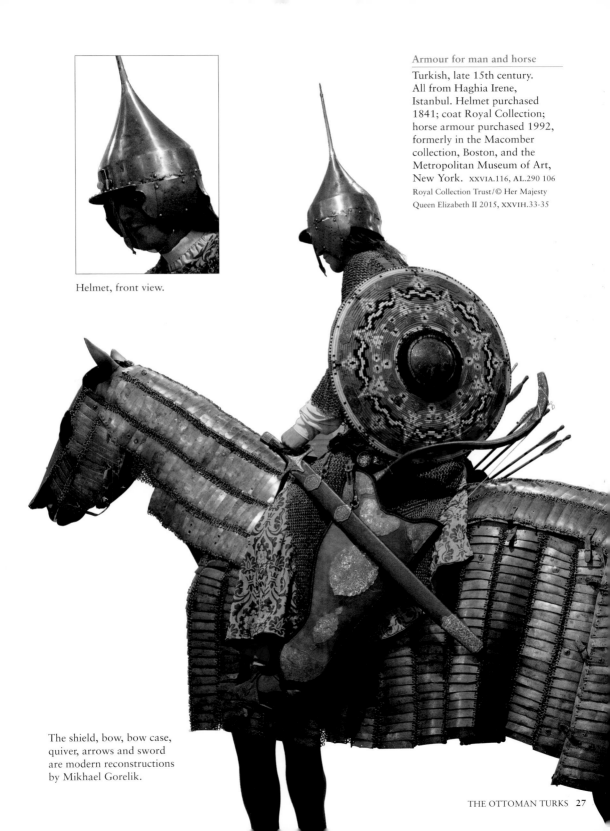

Helmet, front view.

Armour for man and horse

Turkish, late 15th century.
All from Haghia Irene,
Istanbul. Helmet purchased
1841; coat Royal Collection;
horse armour purchased 1992,
formerly in the Macomber
collection, Boston, and the
Metropolitan Museum of Art,
New York. XXVIA.116, AL.290 106
Royal Collection Trust/© Her Majesty
Queen Elizabeth II 2015, XXVIH.33-35

The shield, bow, bow case,
quiver, arrows and sword
are modern reconstructions
by Mikhael Gorelik.

◄ Shaffron (*at alinlici*)

Turkish, 16th century. From the collection of Richard Williams, 1974; from the arsenal of Haghia Irene, Istanbul. XXVIH.17

This shaffron is made of tombak, or gilt copper, which was a popular medium for metalwork in 16th-century Turkey.

▶ Peytral panel

Turkish, late 15th century. Purchased 1989; from the arsenal of Haghia Irene, Istanbul. XXVIH.25

This is a section from the left of the chest portion of a horse armour. Most surviving Ottoman horse armours are plain, but this fragment shows the rich gilding and etching with which some of them were decorated.

Saddle (*eyer*)

Ottoman, probably Algeria or Morocco. Late 18th century. Acquired before 1859. XXVIH.11

This has a saddlecloth of crimson velvet lined with thin leather. The covering is embroidered with gold wire thread, and there is a rosette of thread, gimp, and spangles at the back of the cantle.

END OF AN ERA

The Ottoman Empire expanded under Sulayman the Magnificent (1520–66) to include the whole of Muslim North Africa, Egypt, Syria, the Anatolian homeland, and the Balkan peninsula. This empire even threatened Western Europe: in 1683, Vienna was only just saved from the Turks. But the Ottomans failed to progress and industrialize, and their empire crumbled during the 19th century.

◄ Helmet (çiçak)

Turkish. 16th century.
Purchased 1842 from the
arsenal of Haghia Irene,
Istanbul. XXVIA.115

The whole helmet was
originally covered in gilding,
and is decorated with bands
of calligraphy recording the
titles of an unnamed sultan.
All the original lining
survives; it is very rare to
find a Turkish helmet with
its lining intact.

► Helmet (çiçak)

Turkish, 16th century.
From the collection of
Richard Williams, 1972;
from the arsenal of Haghia
Irene, Istanbul. XXVIA.118

The skull of this helmet is
formed from a European
bacinet skull of the late
14th century.

Helmet

Turkish, probably
17th century. Acquired
before 1859. xxvia.124

This helmet is one of a small
group of helmets of a most
unusual form, made of
leather covered with velvet,
overlaid with a framework
of gilt copper (*tombak*).
They may have been made
for janissary officers.

Kurdish cavalryman,
from Melchior Lorck's
series of engravings of
Turkish costume,
Augsburg 1626. i.959

ARMOUR

Mail defences continued to be used until the 19th century in the Turkish lands. Many had large, riveted links stamped with talismanic quotations from the Qur'an. When mail and plate armour was introduced, defences were developed for the thighs and knees, called *dizçek*. Additionally plate defences for the lower arms and legs were produced. The arm defences or *pazipent* were tubular defences, extended for the elbows at the outer end, made of two plates joined by long hinge pins, and fitted with textile hand defences. The lower leg defences comprise flat plates, slightly shaped and embossed for the calf. There has been much debate about whether these are arm or leg defences. Examples retaining their mail extensions to cover the foot show that they are for the legs. The same form was adopted in Russia, where complete examples survive from the 16th century. Unlike European greaves, Turkish ones protect the outside of the leg only. They were worn only by cavalry, and because the inner side of the boot rested against the saddle it did not need protection. In Turkey, body armour formed of columns of mail and plate were replaced during the 16th century by armours comprising a circular central plate joined by mail to smaller plates covering the sides and shoulders (*zirh gomlek gobekligi*, called 'Krug' or 'pot lids' by collectors today) which were worn over mail shirts.

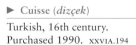

▶ Cuisse (*dizçek*)

Turkish, 16th century. Purchased 1990. XXVIA.194

▶ Greave

Far right: Turkish, late 15th century. Purchased 1842; from the arsenal of Haghia Irene, Istanbul. XXVIA.129

From the rear you can see columns of smaller plates joined by mail.

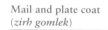

Mail and plate coat (*zirh gomlek*)

Turkish, 16th century. Purchased 1842; from the arsenal of Haghia Irene, Istanbul. XXVIA.14

Detail showing foliage decoration on the plates.

► Breastplate (*zirh gomlek gobekligi*)

Turkish, late 16th century. Purchased 1842; from the arsenal of Haghia Irene, Istanbul. XXVIA.25

An inscription on this piece states that it was owned by a Wazir in 1067 AH (1656/7). The fluted decoration of the piece suggests that it was made some years before that.

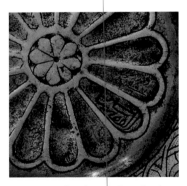

Inscription detail, including the date.

◄ Cuirass (*zirh gomlek gobekligi*)

Turkish, late 16th century. Purchased 1842; from the arsenal of Haghia Irene, Istanbul. XXVIA.27

The bows used by the Ottoman Turks and their predecessors were short, composite recurved bows called *kaman*, made with horn bellies, wooden cores and sinew on the back, with relatively short 'ears' (*siyah* in Arabic, *kasan* in Turkish, the stiffened ends of the arms of the bow that give part of its characteristic performance). The horn component is usually from the horns of water buffalo, antelope, sheep or goat. Maple is the most popular core wood. The sinew is taken from the legs of the same group of ungulates, and attached using fish glue. After the large-scale introduction of firearms, flight archery, shooting very light arrows for maximum distance with specially configured bows, remained a very popular sport among the Turks.

The bow is inscribed at this end with the date, and at the other end with 'made by Uryani-zade'. Flight bows were designed to shoot light arrows great distances, often in excess of 800 paces.

Mounted archer (timariot) from Melchior Lorck's series of engravings of Turkish costume, Augsburg 1626. I.959

Composite flight bow (*kaman*)

Turkish, dated 1254 AH (1838/9). Presented by J. B. Bell Esq. 1978. XXVIB.37

CANNON

The Turks were relatively late adopters of gunpowder weapons. They probably adopted cannon from their Hungarian or Venetian neighbours; they certainly used them at the siege of Antalya in 1424 and certainly had cannon made in Transylvania in the 15th century. At the siege of Constantinople in 1453 bombards played a major role, and from the 15th to the 18th centuries the Turks produced some of the finest guns ever cast, as well as providing skilled artillerists to other parts of the Islamic world. Several of these medieval great guns survived in the forts protecting the straits of the Dardanelles, and one of these was acquired by the Royal Armouries. It is made in two pieces, the chase and the breech, which screw together. Both parts are cast with double mouldings at either end joined by sixteen crosspieces, which form sockets for levers used in screwing and unscrewing the two parts. In the sections adjacent to the end mouldings are cast bands of alternately raised and sunken leaf mouldings. The gun fired stone shot, and five granite shot ranging in diameter from 457–559 mm, probably brought from Turkey with this gun, are in the Royal Armouries collection. The gun was probably made in two parts for ease of transport or casting. In place on the Dardanelles forts, these great guns were mounted on wooden beds with large wooden recoil beds behind them. Bishop Pocock, writing about 1740, recorded 22 bronze guns at Çimenlik, the fort at Çanakkale on the south side of the straits. There were twenty more in the 'castle called Rumeli Eskissar' on the north side.

Great bronze gun

Turkish, dated 1464. XIX.164

The muzzle is cast with a Turkish inscription in relief, *Help, Oh God. The Sultan Mehmed Khan son of Murad, made by Munir 'Ali in the month of Rejeb in the year 868'* for Fatih Sultan Mehmet (1432–81).

Transferred from the Rotunda Museum of Artillery, Woolwich, 1929.
From the battery of the fort of Kilitbahir on the north side of the Dardanelles, presented by Sultan Abdulaziz Han to Queen Victoria in 1866 following negotiations started in 1857 by General (later Sir) J. H. Lefroy.

They were capable of firing right across the straits, a distance of 750 m, and were still working in 1807 when they damaged six of the ships of Sir John Duckworth's squadron when he attempted to force the straits. By 1866 there were only fifteen of the guns left. The earliest recorded one, dated 1458, had recently been broken up. The 1464 gun is the next earliest, and the other dated guns were all made in 1521. It was Ottoman practice in the 15th century to cast these great guns at the sites where they were required, and this practice is recorded at the siege of Constantinople in 1453 and in the first siege of Rhodes in 1480.

Turkish guns were made individually, and had detailed notes regarding their calibre and required powder charge engraved near the breech. The 15th century guns were made both in bronze and wrought iron. Under Sulayman the Magnificent the emphasis shifted towards cast bronze guns only, some, like the cannon illustrated here, with opulent decoration, others made without decoration in the 'plain style' popular in other branches of the Ottoman decorative arts of the period.

Bronze 52-pounder gun

Turkish, dated 1524–5, carriage English, 1802. xix.243

The cast bronze barrel is 16-sided with a flat cascabel. The upper surface is decorated in relief with panels of stylised foliage and scrollwork and has two cartouches framing inscriptions in Arabic, the one near the breech reading *Made by Murad son of Abdullah, Chief Gunner,* the other at the muzzle reading *The Solomon of the Age, the Great Sultan, commanded the Dragon Guns; when they breathe, roaring like thunder, may the enemy's forts be razed to the ground. Year of Hegira 931,* referring to the Sultan Sulayman the Magnificent for whom it was cast. The carriage was made for the gun at Woolwich.

Taken in Egypt in 1801 at the battle of Alexandria, and placed in St. James's Park on 21 March 1802, the anniversary of the battle. This gun, now on Horse Guards Parade, was transferred to the charge of the Armouries from the War Office in 1904.

FIREARMS

Hand firearms were also introduced from Europe, but adopted with enthusiasm by the Turks. One army corps, the Janissaries (*yeniçeri* or 'new troops'), previously armed with composite bows, was armed with matchlock muskets from the early 16th century. This corps was recruited after 1380 by human tax called the *devshirmeh*, in which mostly Christian boys were selected for the unit. They were uniformed, paid, and marched to music. The Turkish matchlock, *fitilli tufek*, had a very simple mechanism in which the trigger was connected to the serpentine by a direct linkage, enabling the smouldering match cord to be lowered very gently onto the priming powder in the pan. They were highly influential, and most of the other matchlocks of Asia followed this design. From 1389 the army also used a conscript system to recruit irregular infantry, the *azabs*.

In the 17th century a type of flintlock mechanism called the miquelet lock became popular in the Ottoman Empire. This type of flintlock is distinguished by having its mainspring on the outside of the lock. Ottoman miquelet lock guns (*çakmakli tufek* or *shishane*) generally had five-sided butts, like those of the earlier matchlocks. The alternative name ('six' in Persian) is thought to refer either to the rifling (though six-grooved rifling is rare), the facets of the butt (though there are five) or the facets of the barrel (which are often hexagonal). Their barrels were Turkish, of pattern-welded steel, fitted with a tower backsight and a leaf foresight, and with rifled barrels. Seven-grooved rifling was popular throughout the empire. Many Ottoman flintlocks were made in the Balkans, and have numerous regional variants. *Shishana* were made in Bosnia, where their stocks were decorated with bone, ivory, silver and brass plaques, and often studded with brass nails.

▼ Trainee janissaries with matchlocks, from Bartholomew von Pezzen's album of scenes from Istanbul, painted between 1586 and 1591. ÖNB/Wien, Cod. 8626, fo. 14v

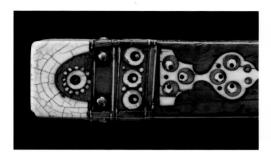

Decoration detail showing ivory inlay.

Muzzle detail showing decorative mouldings and ramrod.

Matchlock musket (*fitilli tufek*)

Turkish, 17th century. Purchased from the A. C. Tirri collection, 2009. XXVIF.241

With a Damascus steel barrel decorated with a kirk nardaban pattern in the watered steel. The stock is of wood, decorated with natural and green stained ivory mosaic cartouches and bands, and the butt plate is of ivory.

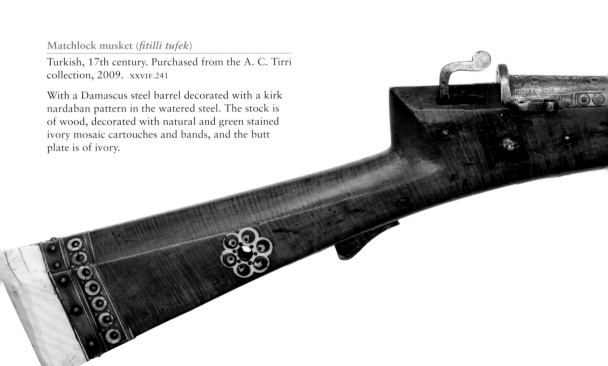

The Herzegovinan *dzerferdar* has a down-curved, slightly flaring stock, and its stock is characteristically covered in mother-of-pearl plaques forming a tessellated design. A similar gun, with the stock covered in brass sheet, is the *çubuklija* (probably after the local long-stemmed pipe). The *arnautka* or *tançika* of south Bosnia and northern Albania has a narrow T-shaped butt (from which its

▲ Baltic lock long-gun (*çakmakli tufek*)

Turkish, 17th century.
XXVIF.179

alternative name is derived), and this and the stock are usually covered in brass sheet, often lavishly decorated. These guns usually have Italian barrels, or were made in Brescia for export.

The *paragun* is north Bosnian, and has a thinned version of the traditional Ottoman stock shape, and has a textile-covered stock (the name is probably derived from a Venetian fabric). The Greek *kariophili*, Serbo-Croat *rasak* ('horns' from the shape of the butt), has a narrow stock flaring to the butt where there is a deep hollow. The stocks of these guns are often covered with decorated brass sheet like the *tançika*.

Barrel detail, showing maker's inscription.

▲ Wheellock musket

Probably Balkan, lock German, mid 17th century. Purchased 1990. XXVIF.178

Only one other Turkish wheellock is known, and that was captured during the Turco-Venetian War of 1645–69. This musket has the maker's name, Rajab, engraved on the barrel. The stock is inlaid with mother-of-pearl plaques, and four cartouches inscribed with Qur'anic inscriptions.

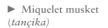

► Miquelet musket
(*tançika*)

Albanian, dated 1792.
Purchased from the Norton
Hall collection with the aid
of the NACF, 1942.
XXVIF.25

► Miquelet rifle
(*çakmakli tufek*)

Turkish, 19th century.
Old Tower collection.
XXVIF.115

▼ Miquelet rifle (*çakmakli tufek*)

Turkish, dated 1220 AH, 1805/6.
Purchased from the Norton Hall
collection with the aid of the
NACF, 1942. XXVIF.5

Lock detail underside.

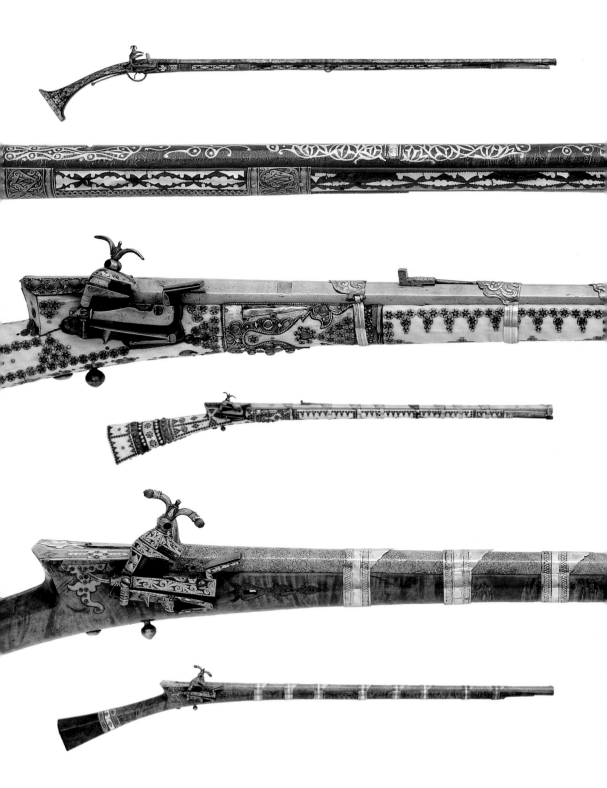

► Miquelet long-guns
(*rasak*)

Balkan, early 18th and
19th century. Purchased
from the Norton Hall
collection with the aid of
the NACF, 1942. XXVIF.9

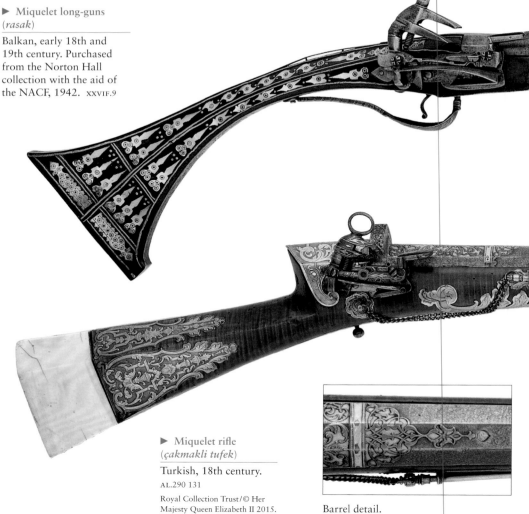

► Miquelet rifle
(*çakmakli tufek*)

Turkish, 18th century.
AL.290 131

Royal Collection Trust / © Her
Majesty Queen Elizabeth II 2015.

Barrel detail.

► Miquelet musket
(*çakmakli tufek*)

Turkish, early 19th century,
by Mahmud Khan.
Purchased from the Norton
Hall collection with the aid
of the NACF, 1942. XXVIF.8

Detail showing
maker's mark.

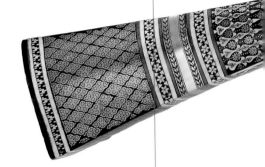

Miquelet lock pistols became popular in the Ottoman Empire in the 18th century. Some, called *ledenica* in Montenegro, *çelina* in Macedonia and other parts of the Balkans, have thin, slightly curved stocks terminating in pointed pear-shaped pommels, and their entire stocks are covered in silver plates cast, engraved and chased in relief. The *zlatka* is of the same form but gilded. The general Turkish word for a pistol is *kubur*, and this is usually applied to imported French or Italian weapons as well as those made in Albanian centres such as Prizren. These guns usually have conventional flintlocks with internal main springs.

▶ Flintlock pistol (*çelina*)

Balkan, 19th century. Purchased from the Norton Hall collection with the aid of the NACF, 1942. XXVIF.16

The stock is covered in cast silver plates, the trigger and guard are chiselled en suite.

▼ Flintlock pistol (*çelina*)

Balkan, early 19th century. Purchased from the Norton Hall collection with the aid of the NACF, 1942. XXVIF.18

▶ One of a pair of holsters (*kuburluk*)

Turkish, late 18th century Acquired before 1859. XXVIH.13

The fronts of these holsters are covered with blue velvet embroidered in gold wire and set with plates of silver gilt. They were carried in pairs in front of the saddle.

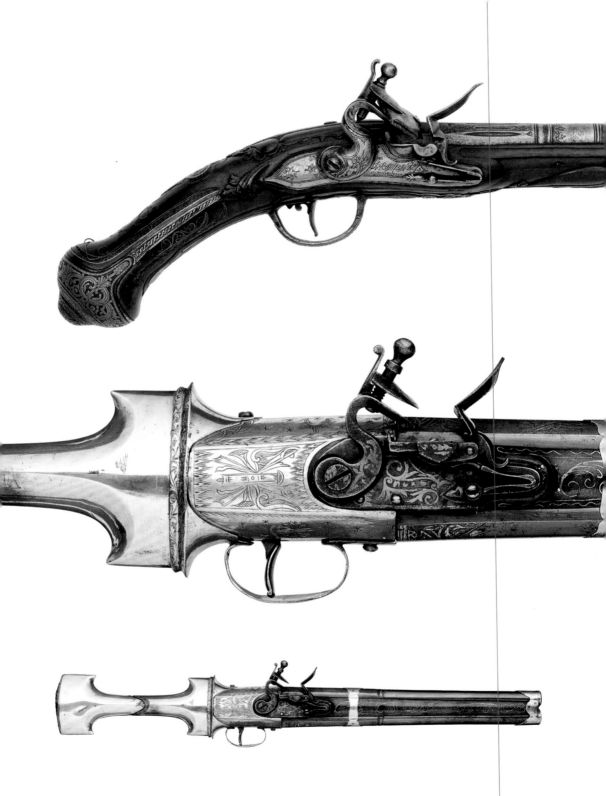

◀ Flintlock pistol (*kubur*)

Early 19th century, Balkan. Purchased from the Norton Hall collection with the aid of the NACF, 1942. XXVIF.21

This pistol has a European-style lock. It is finely engraved, the decoration including meaningless names. The furniture is of iron with heavily overlaid silver scrolls and strap work.

▲ Combined double-barrelled flintlock pistol and dagger

Turkish, Early 19th century. Acquired before 1859. XXVIF.124

The hilt comes apart in the centre to reveal the blade, which is decorated with gold koftgari. The double barrels are discharged at the same time when the flint strikes the steel, and the pan is drilled to give access to the bottom barrel thereby allowing a powder train to each barrel simultaneously.

SWORDS

The Islamic world was famous for its swords. The watered steel of which they were made was of a type and quality well beyond anything available in Europe, and made them objects of great beauty as well as very effective weapons. The curved sword evolved on the eastern steppe around the 10th century, and spread westwards. The characteristic Turkish sword or *kiliç* has a blade which is curved and has a sharpened section of the rear edge towards the point, called a false edge or *yelman*. Earlier examples have a gently curved blade while later ones (from the 18th century) have wider blades, a step at the start of the *yelman* and an angular curve. The hilt was either of pistol-grip form, with a bulbous pommel, usually formed of two horn plates, or with a narrow angled pommel, and a guard formed of straight steel quillons.

▶ Sword (*kiliç*)

Turkish, Court Workshops at Istanbul. About 1560. Purchased 1990. XXVIS.293

This is one of the earliest Ottoman Turkish curved swords to survive. It is closely comparable to the 'Sword of the Scribe of the Prophet', about 1560, (detail below) in the Topkapı Palace Museum, Istanbul TSM 21/141, which still has the precious stones with which our sword was originally inlaid.

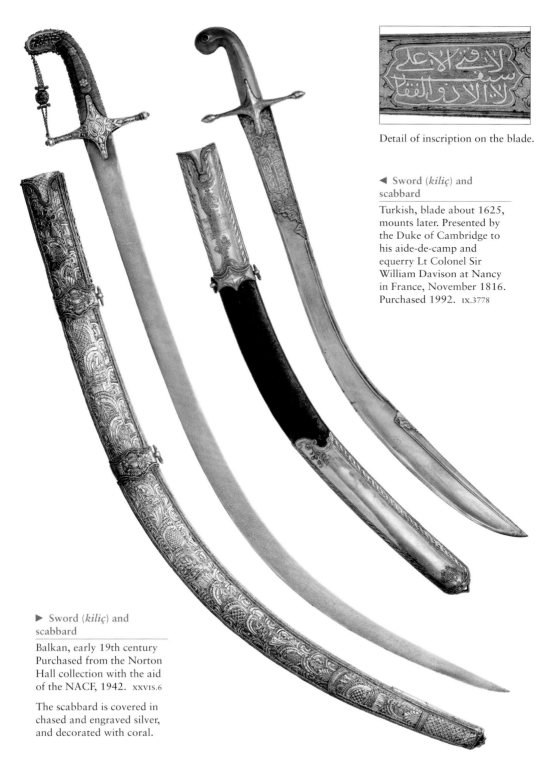

Detail of inscription on the blade.

◀ Sword (*kiliç*) and scabbard

Turkish, blade about 1625, mounts later. Presented by the Duke of Cambridge to his aide-de-camp and equerry Lt Colonel Sir William Davison at Nancy in France, November 1816. Purchased 1992. IX.3778

▶ Sword (*kiliç*) and scabbard

Balkan, early 19th century Purchased from the Norton Hall collection with the aid of the NACF, 1942. XXVIS.6

The scabbard is covered in chased and engraved silver, and decorated with coral.

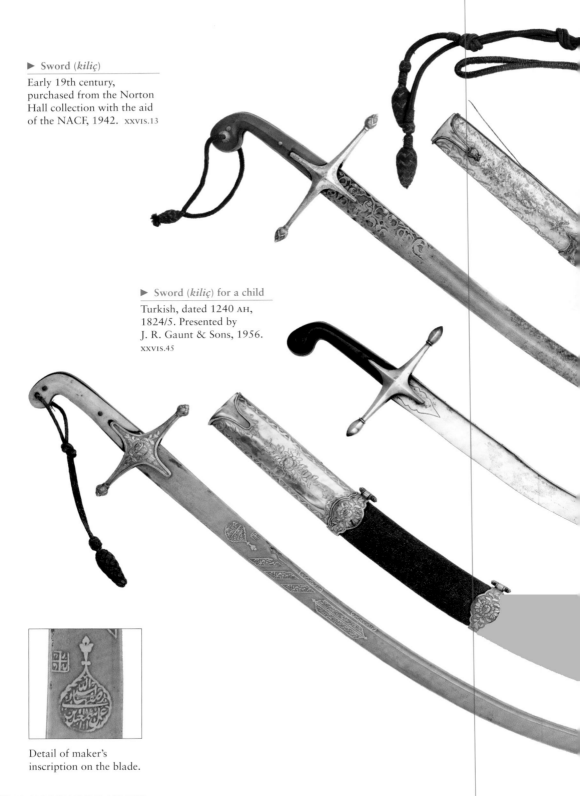

▶ Sword (*kiliç*)

Early 19th century,
purchased from the Norton
Hall collection with the aid
of the NACF, 1942. xxvis.13

▶ Sword (*kiliç*) for a child

Turkish, dated 1240 ʌн,
1824/5. Presented by
J. R. Gaunt & Sons, 1956.
xxvis.45

Detail of maker's
inscription on the blade.

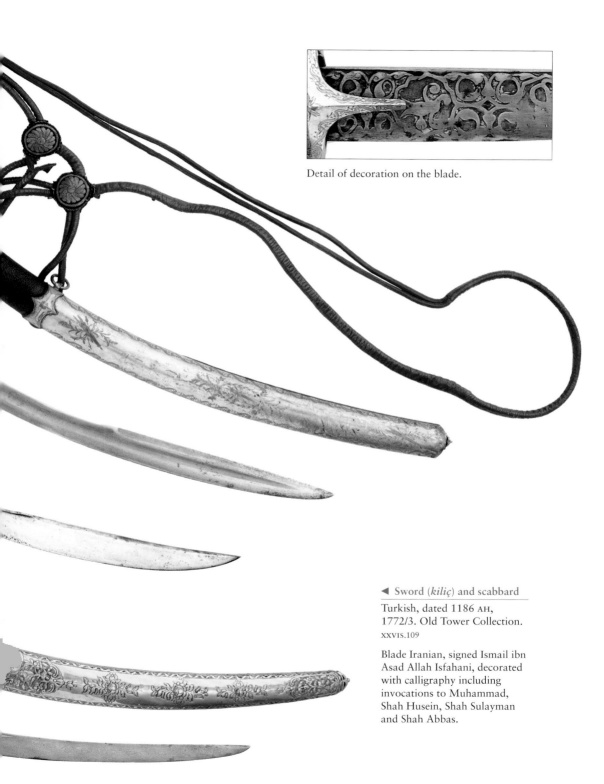

Detail of decoration on the blade.

◄ Sword (*kiliç*) and scabbard

Turkish, dated 1186 AH,
1772/3. Old Tower Collection.
XXVIS.109

Blade Iranian, signed Ismail ibn
Asad Allah Isfahani, decorated
with calligraphy including
invocations to Muhammad,
Shah Husein, Shah Sulayman
and Shah Abbas.

DAGGERS

Another form of sword, a short sword or long dagger, is the *yataghan*. This usually has an eared hilt and a forward curved blade, and may descend from the ancient Macedonian *kopis* or *machaira*, though similar blades and eared hilts are known from bronze daggers from Luristan dateable to about 1300 BC. These first appeared in Turkish service in the late 15th century, and spread throughout the Ottoman Empire. The characteristic type of the middle of the 18th century to the early 19th century have hilts and scabbards covered with silver heavily decorated in relief. The characteristic dagger of the empire is the *hancer*, the Turkish transliteration of the Persian word *khanjar*, generally with a waisted (or 'fiddle-shaped', as Egerton put it) hilt and a curved, double-edged blade.

▶ *Yataghan*

Turkish, dated 1223 AH, 1808/9. Acquired before 1859. XXVIS.105

Signed 'Hasan', with walrus ivory hilt.

▶ *Yataghan* and scabbard

Turkish, 18th century. Acquired from the Dr R. Pace collection, 1964. XXVIS.147

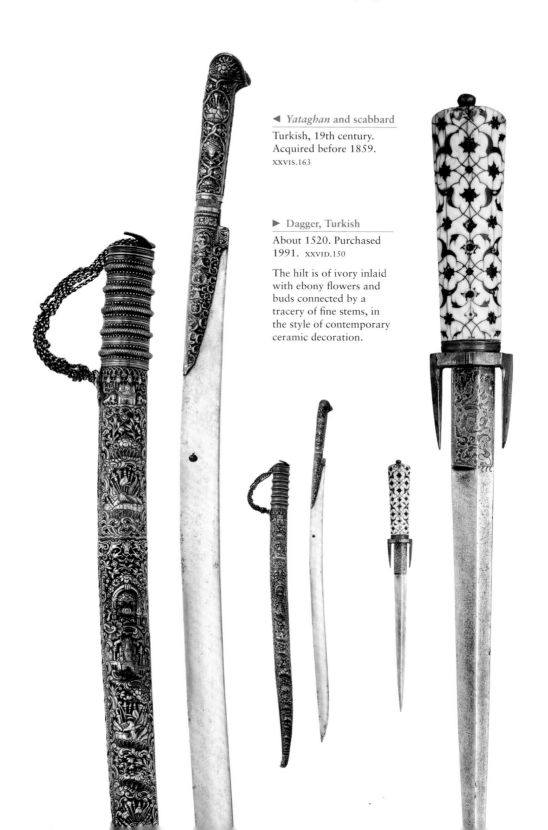

◄ *Yataghan* and scabbard

Turkish, 19th century.
Acquired before 1859.
XXVIS.163

► Dagger, Turkish

About 1520. Purchased
1991. XXVID.150

The hilt is of ivory inlaid
with ebony flowers and
buds connected by a
tracery of fine stems, in
the style of contemporary
ceramic decoration.

► *Hancer* and scabbard

Turkish, early 19th century. Purchased from the Norton Hall collection with the aid of the NACF, 1942. XXVID.2

The pistol shaped grip is of green jade carved in low relief with foliage and lotus flowers.

► Far right: *Kard* and scabbard

Turkish, early 19th century. Purchased from the Norton Hall collection with the aid of the NACF, 1942. XXVID.4

The walrus ivory grip has a mount of nielloed silver set with a band of turquoises.

DECORATION

Islamic arms and armour were also characterised by their opulent decoration. Swords with blades of watered 'Wootz' steel produced in the Middle East were thought in Europe to originate from Damascus, and are often known as 'Damascus' swords today. The same term is applied to gun barrels made of pattern-welded steel, where two or more steel bars of different alloys are twisted and forged together to produce a naturally striped surface. The same city also gave its name to two techniques of decoration with gold, both called 'Damascening'; one in which gold wire was hammered into a groove chiselled into the surface of the metal ('true' Damascening or gold inlay) and another in which gold wire was hammered onto a file hatched surface ('false' Damascening or gold overlay, called *koftgari* in India). In addition to these forms of gilding, arms were frequently set with precious or semi-precious stones, and lined with opulent textiles such as silks and velvets.

▼ Sword (*kiliç*) and detail from the blade showing damascening. xxvis.109

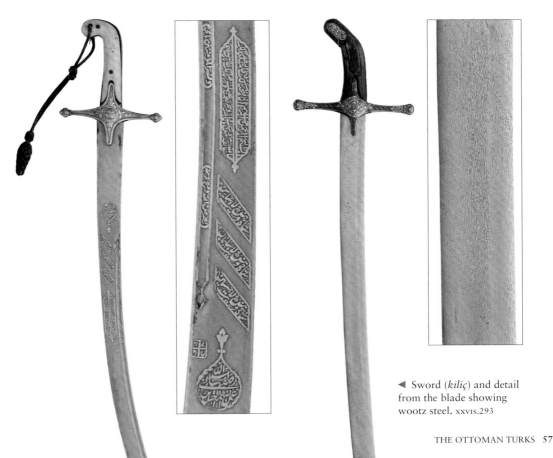

◄ Sword (*kiliç*) and detail from the blade showing wootz steel. xxvis.293

THE ARABIAN PENINSULA

The Arabian Peninsula has remained the heart of the Islamic world from the foundation of the Umayyad Empire to the present day. The Hajj, the annual pilgrimage to Mecca that all Muslims should undertake during their lives, is thought to have evolved from a pre-Islamic pilgrimage. Muhammad's return with his followers from Medina to Mecca in 631, and the cleansing and re-consecration of the Kaaba that followed, established it as one of the pillars of Islam.

◄ Hilt detail, dagger (*khanjar*) Arabian, Oman, early 19th century. XXVID.41

▼ The Arabian Peninsula.

DAGGERS

The arms of the Arabian Peninsula have retained a character distinct from the rest of the Islamic world. The Arabic word *khanjar* is a general term for most of the daggers of the Muslim world, but refers in the sheikdoms of the east coast to a particular type of dagger with a double-edged, angularly curved blade. They are characterised by lavish use of silver, both wire and filigree in their decoration. Others have wooden hilts decorated in gold, with gold coins. Omani *khanjar* are traditionally carried on a belt, decorated in silver like the dagger, and permanently attached to the scabbard by a complex of silver wires, loops and knops. Some areas have particular words for their own dagger types. *Janbiyya* (literally 'worn at the side') is often used (inaccurately) for any Islamic dagger, but it is only properly used for daggers from Yemen and western Arabia, while *khanjar* is used on the east coast, particularly in Oman. The daggers of western and southern Arabia have quite different hilts from those of the east coast, and have none of the lavish silver mountings. One in the Royal Armouries collection has a simple hilt of giraffe horn. Among the Bedouin, the term *giddamiyah* is used.

Hilt detail.

▶ Dagger (*janbiyya*)
Arabian, Yemen, probably late 19th century. Transferred from the Glencorse Museum, Edinburgh, 1991. XXVID.154

▼ Dagger (*khanjar*)
with scabbard and belt

Arabian, possibly
Muscat or Oman,
19th century.
Transferred from the
Glencorse Museum,
Edinburgh, 1991.
XXVID.153

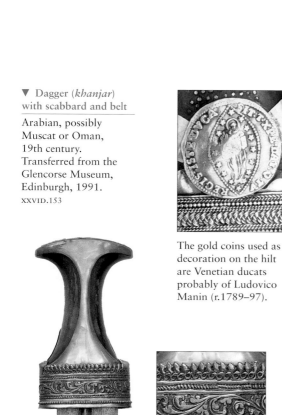

The gold coins used as
decoration on the hilt
are Venetian ducats
probably of Ludovico
Manin (r.1789–97).

Hilt detail.

◄ Dagger (*khanjar*)
and scabbard

Arabian, Oman,
early 19th century.
XXVID.41

SWORDS AND FIREARMS

In Oman a straight, double-edged sword with a long, tapering, guardless hilt is used (the *kattara*). Because of Omani trading contacts across the Indian Ocean, these swords are found in other places linked with Oman, and are often called Zanzibar swords. These usually have imported German blades, and those in the Royal Armouries collection are marked, one with the 'running wolf' of Solingen, the other with adorsed crescents. Another form of sword found all over Arabia is the *saif*, the standard Arabic word for sword, with a characteristic notched grip and down turned pommel. Like the Omani swords, many of these have imported European blades.

► Sword (*saif*) and scabbard

Arabian, early 19th century. Lord Hardinge of Penshurst, 1955.
XXVIS.37

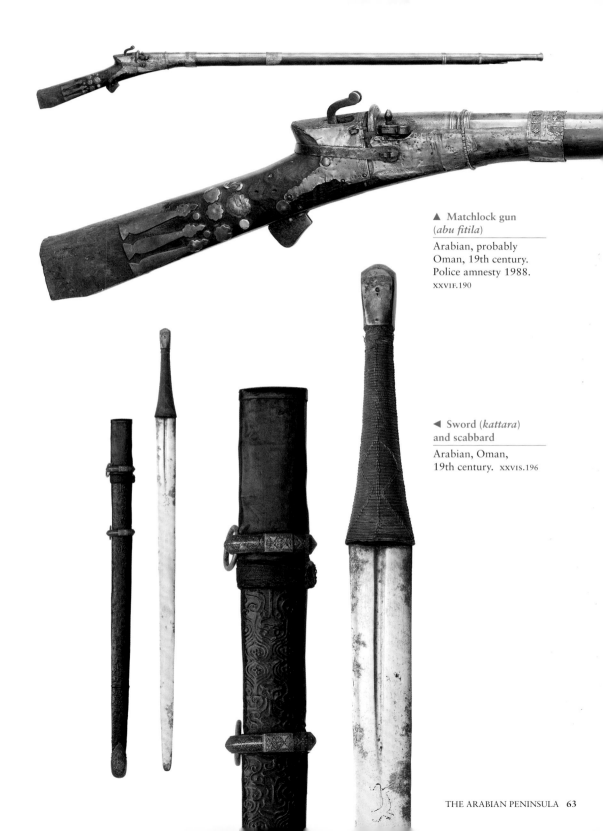

▲ Matchlock gun
(*abu fitila*)

Arabian, probably
Oman, 19th century.
Police amnesty 1988.
XXVIF.190

◄ Sword (*kattara*)
and scabbard

Arabian, Oman,
19th century. XXVIS.196

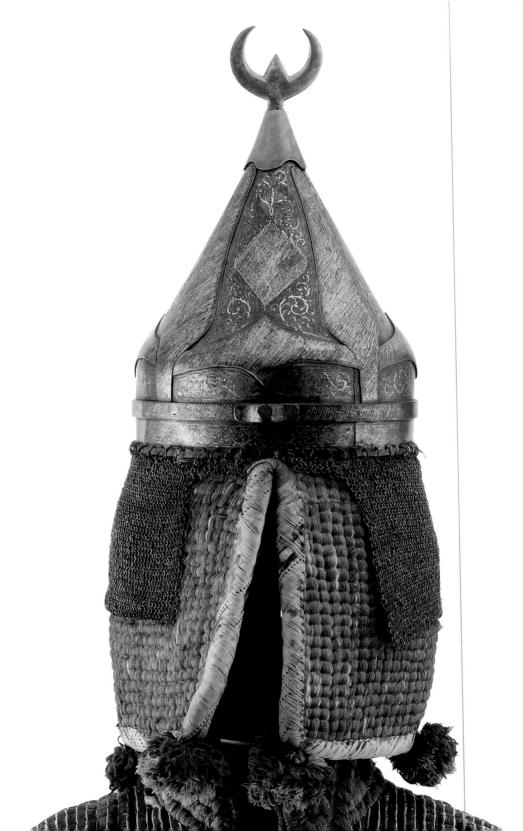

ISLAMIC KINGDOMS OF NORTH AFRICA

The spread of Islam from Syria through Egypt and across the coastal regions of North Africa occurred under the Ummayad Caliphate in the late 7th century. The Berbers of north-west Africa were early converts, and provided much of the Umayyad army which conquered Spain in the early 8th century. The religion spread southwards gradually, into Sudan and the Bornu kingdom of the western Sahara in the 11th century. By the 16th century the kingdom of Kano was Muslim, and the Sokhoto Caliphate of Nigeria was also part of the Islamic world by the early 19th century. The Ottoman Empire at its greatest extent in the 17th century included the whole of the North African seaboard. Little is known of the arms and armour of Africa before the 19th century. Great quantities of material were brought back to Europe as souvenirs during and after the colonial wars, and it is from this that what knowledge we have is largely drawn.

◀ Helmet, Sudanese, 19th century. XXVIA.191

▼ North Africa.

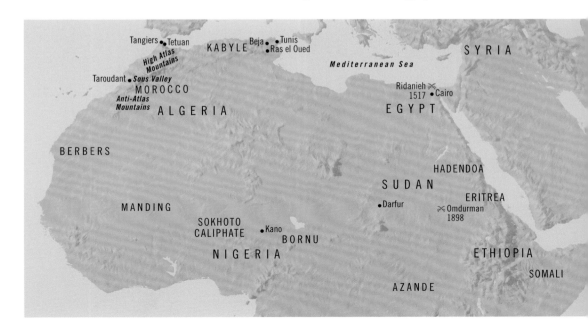

SWORDS

The characteristic sword of the eastern Sahara and the Sudan is the *kaskara*. It has a straight, usually double-edged blade, and the hilt has an iron cross-guard with slightly flaring langets above and below. The broad similarity between this and the medieval European sword leads to constant confusion between the two types. Many of the blades for these swords were imported along the trade routes into Africa, either from Spain or Germany, and the European

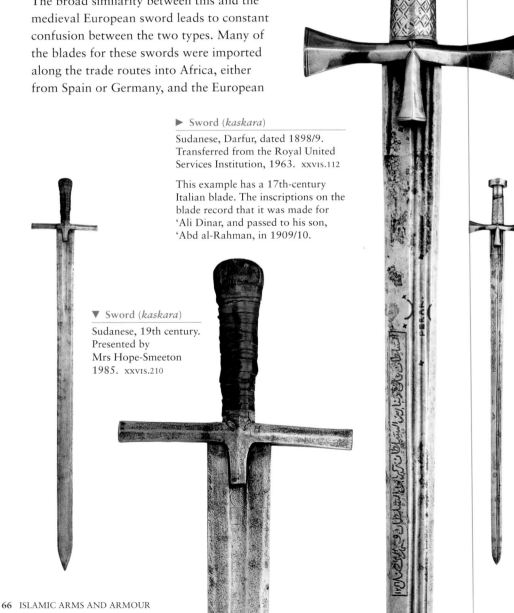

▶ Sword (*kaskara*)

Sudanese, Darfur, dated 1898/9. Transferred from the Royal United Services Institution, 1963. XXVIS.112

This example has a 17th-century Italian blade. The inscriptions on the blade record that it was made for 'Ali Dinar, and passed to his son, 'Abd al-Rahman, in 1909/10.

▼ Sword (*kaskara*)

Sudanese, 19th century. Presented by Mrs Hope-Smeeton 1985. XXVIS.210

marks they bear, commonly the crescent moon and sun in splendour, or the orb and cross, add to the confusion. The scabbards for these swords flare to a leaf-shaped chape; the shape is supposed to derive from the use of crocodile skins for the covering of the wooden former. The finest *kaskara* were made for the Sultan 'Ali Dinar of Darfur (1898–1916). These swords were fitted with a mixture of European export blades and locally made blades, but all were fitted with fine silver or silver-gilt hilts, and lavishly inscribed with the circumstances of their manufacture and subsequent provenance.

◄▼ Swords (*kaskara*)

Sudanese, Darfur, 19th century. XXVIS.165, 166

Both of these swords have silver mounted hilts decorated with the embossed work of the swordsmiths of Darfur.

In the central Sahara another cross-hilted sword was used by the Tuareg, called the *takouba*. It is easily distinguished from the *kaskara*, having a narrower and deeper cross-guard, formed of wood and leather. The blades of these swords are shorter than those of the eastern Saharan swords. Further west, on the fringes of the Sahara, the Manding people used a short curved sword, with a guardless hilt covered in leather and a matching scabbard, usually decorated with fringes of leather thongs where the scabbard joins the baldrick. An unusual type of dagger is found in this area, particularly in Chad and southern Libya, the arm-knife, *telek* or *loi-bo*, so called because it is carried on the forearm,

▶ Sword (*flyssa*)

Moroccan, Kabyle, 19th century
XXVIS.62

▶ Sword (*nimcha*) and scabbard

Far right: Moroccan, dated 1835/6 (1251 AH). Transferred from the Royal Collection, 1954.
XXVIS.103

by a loop attached to the scabbard throat. The loop on the scabbard fits round the arm, enabling the knife to be carried conveniently. These knives are also called 'robe knives', as they are covered by the sleeve of the robe.

The Kabyle Berbers of northern Algeria have a characteristic sword called a *flyssa*, which has a straight, single-edged blade which swells at the centre then narrows to a long point, and which is fitted with a guardless hilt with a pommel in the form of a stylised camel head, usually of brass. The sword of the coastal kingdom of Morocco is the *nimcha*, a sabre with a curved single-edged blade and a notched hilt with forward curving quillons, almost indistinguishable from the Arabian *saif*. These frequently have European blades, mostly French.

Tuareg warrior wearing a takouba.
Roger Balsom

◄ Manding sword

Mid 19th century.
Purchased 1986 xxvis.206

► Arm knife (*loi-bo*) and scabbard

African, Somali, late 19th century. xxvid.137

The matching Moroccan dagger is the *koummya*, with a double-edged, curved blade with most of the concave edge but only half of the convex edge sharpened, and a long, slender hilt formed of horn, ivory or bone panels with a lunate pommel, the scabbard and mounts usually of brass and silver with engraved and chased decoration. The *koummya* used by the Berbers of the High Atlas Mountains has an extreme form with a very large pommel.

A most unusual sword type is found in Ethiopia, the *shotel*, characterised by a forward-curved blade, that is, one with the edge on the inside of the curve. It is thought that it has a very long history, and that it may be related to the *khepesh* of ancient Egypt. Curiously, *shotel* manufactured for export in England by Wilkinson's have their edges on the outside of the curve. A characteristic dagger of the region, associated with the Hadendoa of Eritrea is the X-hilted dagger of the Beja, with its X-shaped horn hilt and blades either curved, hooked or straight, and double-edged.

▶ Swords and scabbards

Tunisian, about 1850. Purchased from the Great Exhibition, 1851. XXVIs.104, 114

Swords with Tunisian provenances are very rare. They have horn hilts of different types, the H-shaped example being related to Tuareg dagger hilts.

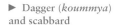

▶ Dagger (*koummya*)
and scabbard

African, Algeria, 19th
century. Presented by
Donald MacAlistair, 1960.
XXVID.42

▶ Dagger (*koummya*)
and scabbard

Far right: African, Morocco,
about 1835. AL.290 130

SPECTRS

The other offensive arms used in this area are spears of huge variety. The best known of these are the *assagais*; the name is the Portuguese and Spanish version of the Berber Arabic *az-zaghayah*, a short throwing or thrusting spear. The term appears in English as early as 1325, and was used for all the spears of this type in the continent. The all-steel spear of the Tuareg, traditionally used from camel back, has a spatulate head and is called the *allarh*. It is used in conjunction with a large rectangular shield called the *ayar*, made of oryx skin. Similar barbed spears of all-iron construction were used in southern Sudan, associated with the Azande and called *baasoo*.

ARMOUR

The great bulk of the body defences surviving from Saharan Africa, called *jibbah*, are not armour at all, but coats of cotton decorated with appliqué panels of coloured fabric. Most of the surviving examples in Britain were brought back from the Omdurman campaign of 1898, and indeed the term *jibbah* first appears in English in connection with the Mahdists in the 1890s.

True armours were, however, produced in this area. Most of them are of quilted cotton, decorated like the Mahdist *jibbahs* with coloured panels. These were either worn on their own or in combination with shirts of riveted mail. The conical helmets which appear with these armours, often decorated with overall gilding, are fitted with deep quilted fabric aventails, often overlaid with mail.

'A skirmish in Abyssinia, Beni-Amer Arabs, in cotton-quilted armour, repulsing an attack by Abyssinians under Ras-Allula on Senhit', from *The Graphic*, 1885.

Many of these helmets are very old indeed, and provide the main source of surviving Mamluk Egyptian helmets of the 15th and 16th century. The mail, too, is often very old, though the manufacture of riveted mail continued at Omdurman into the 1940s. It is likely that the defeat of the Mamluks of Egypt by the Ottomans at the battle of Ridanieh in 1517 released a large quantity of arms and armour into the Sudan and neighbouring regions.

The shields produced in Ethiopia and the Sudan are of a particular form, usually of leather, with a deep, broad cone turned at its rim into a deep flange. Some are plain, and made of rhinoceros hide. Others are larger, and decorated with numerous small plates of silver or silvered copper.

Most of the armours belonged to the cavalry in the Saharan armies, and there is some evidence of the use of horse armour from Bornu in central Sudan, to the south of the desert, and one quilted armour at least survives. Cavalry made up a major component of these armies, together with large quantities of infantry of variable quality and fighting expertise.

◀ Fabric coat (*jibbah*) and helmet

Sudanese, 19th century.
Purchased 1965. xxviA.104, 191

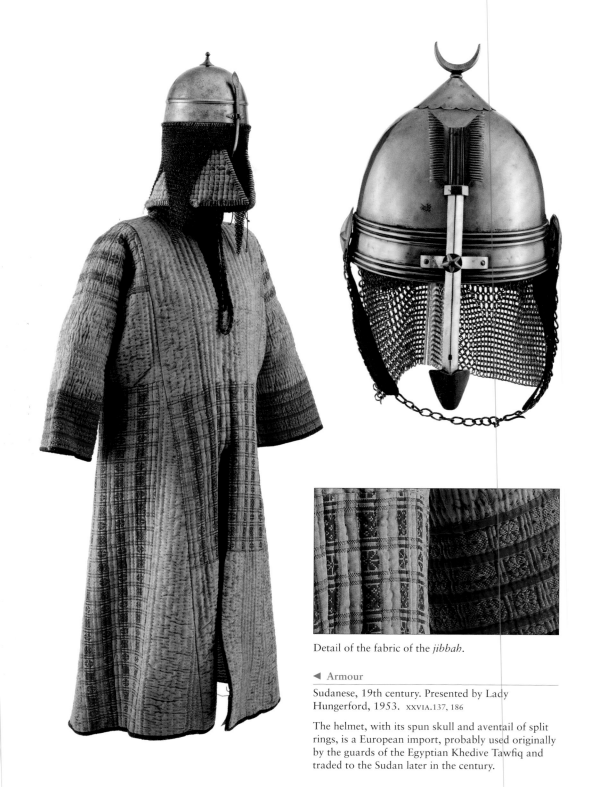

Detail of the fabric of the *jibbah*.

◀ Armour

Sudanese, 19th century. Presented by Lady Hungerford, 1953. XXVIA.137, 186

The helmet, with its spun skull and aventail of split rings, is a European import, probably used originally by the guards of the Egyptian Khedive Tawfiq and traded to the Sudan later in the century.

IRAN AND IRAQ

The Safavid dynasty in Iran (1501–1732) probably arose from Kurdish origins, supported by Turkmen tribes. It was the first non-Mongol dynasty to rule in Persia since the Mongol conquest in the 13th century. In the 16th century the Safavids lost much of their western territory to the Ottoman Turks who used more modern firearms. In the early 18th century Afghan invasions threw Iran into chaos. This was relieved briefly under Nadir Shah (1736–47). He reunified Persia and reconquered much of modern Pakistan from the weakened Mughals, but further chaos followed his death. Iran was reunited again first under the Zands (1750–94) who were descended from lowly Persian soldiers, and then under the Turkmen Qajars (1774–1924).

◀ Battle scene Safavid dynasty, Iran, Qazvin, about 1575.

▼ Iran and Iraq.

ARMOUR

Most of the surviving armour of later Iran was made in the Zand and Qajar periods (1750–1924). However, a small amount of Safavid material survives. In the late 17th century, mail and plate body armour was replaced by a form of plate armour called *chahar a'ineh*, 'four mirrors', comprising four rectangular plates joined by straps worn on the chest over a mail shirt. These were usually decorated with gold over lay, usually with calligraphic passages from the *Qur'an*, and particularly during the Qajar period, with hunting scenes. They were made en suite with a pair of arm defences (*bazuband*), a helmet with a mail aventail and nasal defence (*kolah khod*) and steel shield (*separ*). Riveted mail continued to be made in Iran until the 18th century, when the proliferation of firearms on the battlefield made armour in general, and mail in particular, redundant. The traditional form of armour continued to be made and worn for parades, and, at the end of the 19th century, for sale to European tourists.

Pair of arm defences (*bazuband*)

Iranian, dated 1112 AH (1700/1) AL.290 111-112

The pair are decorated with embossed panels of calligraphy (the Throne Verse from the *Qur'an* II.255) and floral design.

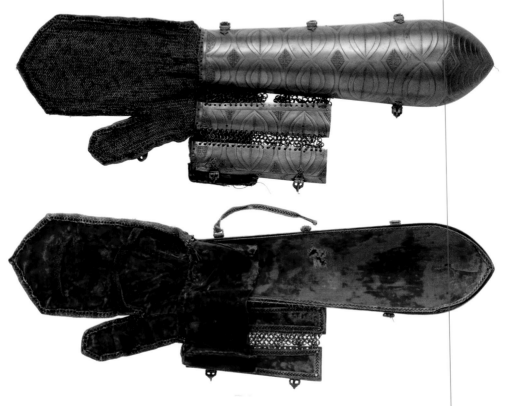

Detail of inscription.

Cuirass (*chahar a'ineh*)

Iranian, dated 1213 AH (1798). Acquired before 1859. XXVIA.72

The four copper plates are decorated with gold lacquer and enamelled flowers. The inscription in Persian at the top of the breastplate reads: *the noble Ghulam 'Ali Khan. Made by the humble 'Ali of Isfahan in the month of Shaban in the year 1213.*

▲ *Chahar a' ineh*.

One panel of the *chahar a' ineh*.

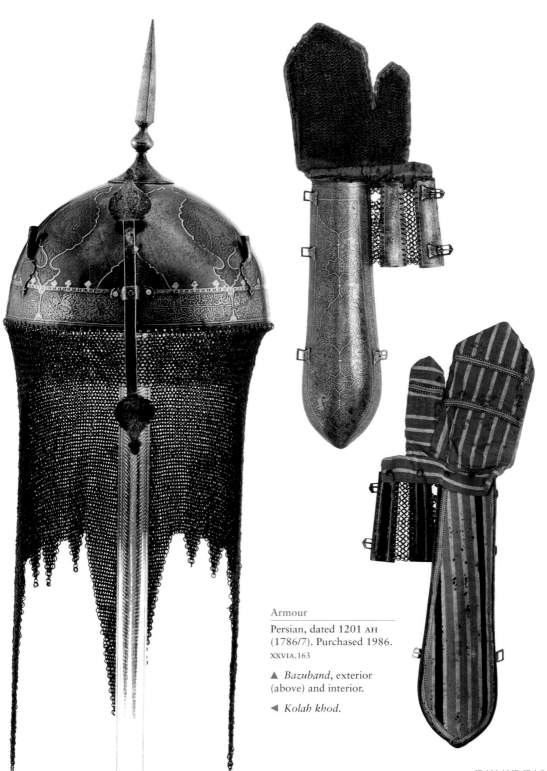

Armour

Persian, dated 1201 AH
(1786/7). Purchased 1986.
XXVIA.163

▲ *Bazuband*, exterior
(above) and interior.

◀ *Kolah khod*.

Helmet (*kolah khod*)

Iranian, early 19th century. Transferred from the Royal Collection, 1954. XXVIA.67

Matching helmet (*kolah khod*) and shield (*separ*)

Iranian, 19th century. Acquired before 1870.
XXVIA.130a–b

SWORDS

Sword blades made in Iran were formed from a watered crucible 'wootz' steel. The characteristic surface is caused by crystallisation of the steel in the crucible in which it was smelted. A super-high carbon steel, it combines flexibility and resilience, and is capable of taking a very fine edge. Persian blades are usually single-edged,

◀ Sword (*shamshir*) and scabbard

Iranian, 18th century. Presented by J. R. Gaunt & Son Ltd, 1956. XXVIS.46

Scabbard detail.

▶ Sword (*shamshir*)
and scabbard

Iranian, 18th century.
Purchased, 1981.
XXVIS.192

with a strong, even curve. Persian *shamshir* blades had a very high reputation and were widely exported both to other parts of the Islamic world and to Europe. One 17th-century sword maker, Asad Allah of Isfahan, had a great reputation, to the extent that his signature was applied to blades for nearly 200 years after his death, and an Asad Allah blade became a byword for a high-quality Iranian blade.

Detail of blade signed Assad Allah of Isfahan.

▶ Sword (*shamshir*)
and scabbard

Iranian, 18th century.
Purchased, 1980.
XXVIS.177

DAGGERS

The usual form of dagger used in Iran and Iraq was the *khanjar*, with a curved, double-edged blade. The hilts were usually waisted, often of steel or of walrus ivory, sometimes of jade and set with semi-precious stones. Lapis lazuli and turquoise were popular in the north and east of Iran.

▼ Dagger (*khanjar*) and scabbard

Iranian, 19th century. Presented by D. Bernhard Smith 1971. XXVID.60

▶ Dagger (*khanjar*)

Iranian, 19th century. Old Tower Collection. XXVID.64

The carved walrus ivory hilt is decorated with a four line Persian verse: *Shining is the sharp blade/ Its name is yataghan/ That which splits a thorn/ Is the amazing khanjar*

► Dagger (*khanjar*) and scabbard

Iranian, 19th century. Presented by the Longsands College, St Neots, 1993.
XXVID.161

This blade is of a rare and unusual type, probably inspired by the cloven point of the Sword of the Prophet. The point is split and formed into five small blades, the centre one swollen into an armour-piercing type.

▼ Knife (*kard*) and scabbard

East Iranian, 18th century. Acquired before 1859.
XXVID.63

HAND-TO-HAND WEAPONS

The large quantity of armour used by cavalry in the Iranian armies led to the popularity of hand-to-hand weapons other than the sword; the mace and the saddle axe. Maces (*gorz*) were popular as symbols of status as well as rank among several Central Asia peoples, and were part of the armoury of the Sassanian cavalry. The most popular type was a flanged mace, usually with six flanges. The saddle axe (*tabarzin*) was a steppe weapon, associated with the Scythians in the ancient period. Many Safavid saddle axes were of very high quality, and signed by their makers, among whom Lutf 'Ali was a particular saddle-axe specialist working in the 17th century.

Axe head (*tabar*)

Iranian, dated 1650.
Purchased 1990.
XXVIC.67

◄ Mace (*gorz*)

Iranian, 18th century.
AL.290 128
Royal Collection Trust / © Her
Majesty Queen Elizabeth II 2015

► Axe (*tabarzin*)

Iranian, 19th century.
Transferred from Bristol
City Museum and Art
Gallery, 1966. XXVIC.5

BOWS

The bow remained the primary weapon of the Iranian cavalry until the widespread introduction of firearms. Called *kaman*, it is a recurved composite bow closely related to the Turkish bow. Like most Asian composite bows it was shot using a thumb release, in which the bowstring is held by the thumb, which is gripped in place by the index finger; a thumb ring is usually worn on the right thumb to facilitate the release. In the 18th and 19th centuries hunting with the bow on horseback remained a popular sport in Iran, and many surviving bows are decorated with hunting scenes.

▲ Archer's thumb ring

Top: Possibly Iranian, bronze, 17th century.
XXVIB.177

► Composite bow (*kaman*)

Iranian, 18th century.
AL.290 122

Royal Collection Trust / © Her Majesty Queen Elizabeth II 2015

Detail of decoration on the bow.

◄ Pair of javelins and case (*jarid*)

Iranian, 18th century. Acquired before 1859. XXVII.223

Pairs of javelins called *jarid* were carried by some mounted troops, and were effective weapons at close quarters. They were constructed with hafts of wood or iron and were carried in a case which was hung from the saddle bow.

Two soldiers of Shah 'Abbas, Persian, late 16th century.

Indian drawings 12 © The University of Manchester

THE CAUCASUS

Armenia in the south was an independent kingdom from 600 BC under the Orontids, and adopted Christianity in 301 AD. It retained independence under the Islamic caliphate as the Bagratid Kingdom, which was conquered by the Byzantines in 1045. After that Armenia was conquered in turn by the Seljuq Turks in 1071 (at the famous battle of Manzikert), and by the Mongols and their successor kingdoms from the 1230s until 1500, when it was divided between Ottoman Turkey and Safavid Persia. In 1915 the Armenians suffered the Armenian genocide at the hands of the Turks. In 1917 the Russians invaded, and Armenia became part of the Transcaucasian Socialist Federative Joint Republic (TSFSR) in 1924. Independent in 1991, it waged the Nagorno-Karabakh war with Azerbaijan until 1994.

◄ Tartar helmet possibly for the Nogai Horde. XXVIA.331

▼ The Caucasus.

Georgia in the west was a Roman client kingdom from 66, Christian from 319 or 337. Named either after its patron saint or its famous farmlands (Greek *georgos*, 'farmer') it grew into an independent medieval kingdom, with a capital at Tblisi. Tblisi was captured by the Umayyads in 645 but became independent of the Abbasids in 813, and remained so until annexed by Russia in 1801. It revolted against Soviet rule but was brutally repressed and incorporated into the TSFSR in 1924. Independent in 1991, it saw government change in the Rose Revolution of 2003.

Azerbaijan in the east was an Achaemenid and Sassanid Persian vassal state, called Albania. In the 7th century it was incorporated into the Umayyad Caliphate, then invaded by the Turkic Oghuz in the 11th century, forming part of the Ghaznavid kingdom. In the 15th century it became part of Shirvanshah, a vassal kingdom of Timurids, and subsequently part of the Zand and Qajar dynasties of Iran. Incorporated into the Russian Empire in 1813, Azerbaijan declared independence in 1918 but was invaded by the Red Army in 1920 and in 1922 became part of the TSFSR. Independent in 1991 it waged the Nagorno-Karabakh war with Armenia until 1994, while the northern section of the old Albania became independent as Daghestan.

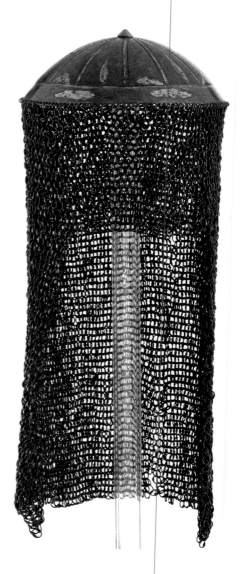

ARMOUR

Mail armour continued to be worn by the cavalry of the region until the 19th century, and a distinctive form of mail hood, called a *misiourka*, with a circular plate at the apex was popular.

▶ Helmet (*misiourka*)

Probably Georgian, 18th century. Acquired before 1859. XXVIA.61

Armour of this type is shown in series of photographs of Khevsur warriors dating from the 1870s to the early 20th century.

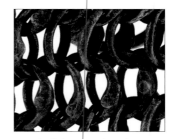

Detail of the riveted mail construction.

▲ Tartar helmet possibly for the Nogai Horde

North Daghestan or southern Ukraine, late 16th century. XXVIA.331

▶ Dagger (*kindjal*) and scabbard

Caucasus, 19th century. XXVID.40

◀ Dagger (*kindjal*) and scabbard

Caucasus, 19th century. XXVID.39

DAGGERS

The most popular type of dagger throughout the region was the *kindjal* or *qama*. This has a straight, double-edged blade with asymmetrical fullers at either side, and a guardless hilt usually formed of horn plates secured through the tang with decorative rivets. The blades are usually pattern-welded.

SWORDS AND FIREARMS

The distinctive sword of the region was the *shasqa*, a sabre with a curved, single-edged blade and a guardless hilt with an eared pommel like that of a *yataghan*.

The firearms of the region were closely related to those of the Ottoman Empire. Rifles with miquelet locks were made in Daghestani centres of Kharbuk, which specialised in barrel making, and Kubachi which specialised in mountings and decoration. Miquelet lock pistols were also popular, and are characterised by their ball butts of walrus ivory. All the arms of the Caucasus are frequently decorated with *niello*, a glossy black alloy of silver, copper, sulphur and lead, usually inlaid and fused with heat into silver alloy sheet. Ramrods were carried separately from the pistols, and worn around the neck.

▶ Miquelet lock pistol
Caucasus, early 19th
century. XXVIF.158

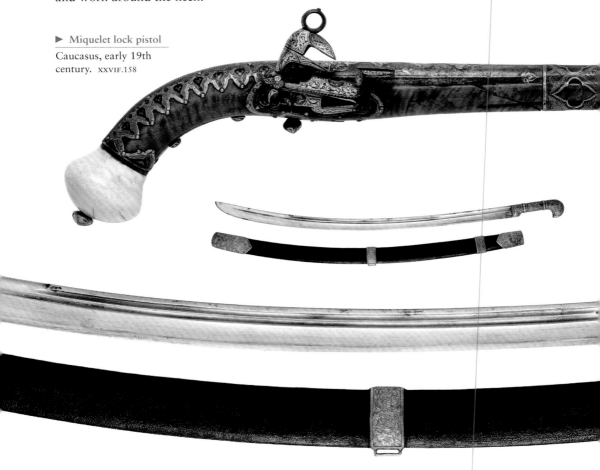

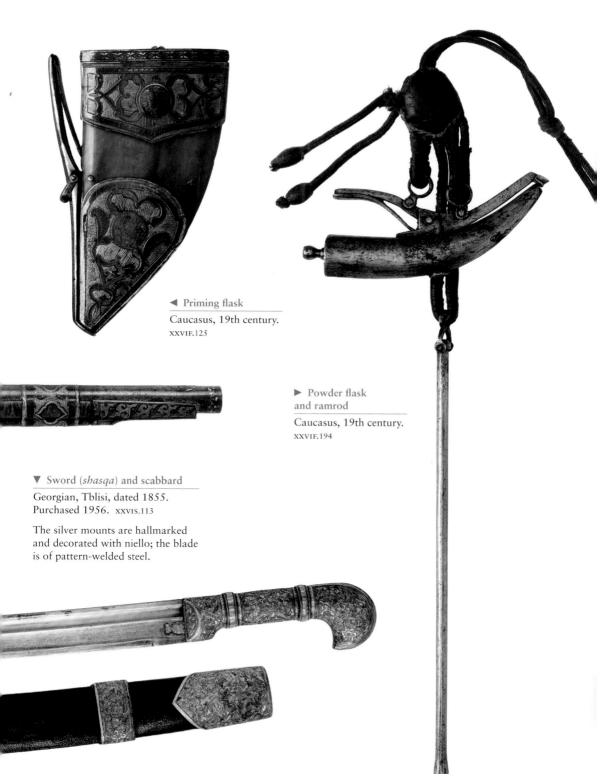

◄ Priming flask
Caucasus, 19th century.
XXVIF.125

► Powder flask
and ramrod
Caucasus, 19th century.
XXVIF.194

▼ Sword (*shasqa*) and scabbard
Georgian, Tblisi, dated 1855.
Purchased 1956. XXVIS.113

The silver mounts are hallmarked
and decorated with niello; the blade
is of pattern-welded steel.

AFGHANISTAN

A fghanistan occupies a key location at the end of the Silk Road, the land route connecting China to Iran and India. As such it was keenly fought over, especially by the horse archer peoples of Central Asia, the Saka, Kushans and Hephthalite or White Huns. It was part of the Sassanid Empire at the time of the Conquest, conquered by the Umayyads in the 7th century, and became fully Islamicised under the Ghaznavid dynasty in the 11th century. Devastated by the Mongol invasions of the 13th century, it was revived under the Ghurids and Timurids as a centre of art and culture. Babur, founder of the Mughal Empire in India, started as a minor ruler in Afghanistan. The modern state dates to the foundation of the Durrani Empire in 1747, with its capital at Khandahar then at Kabul. The empire at its height in the late 19th century incorporated many former Mughal areas in the north of India.

◀ Sword (*pulouar*) and scabbard. xxvis.180

▼ Afghanistan.

SWORDS

The Persian *shamshir* is one of two main forms of sword found in Afghanistan under the Durranis. Afghan made *shamshir* hilts have a Central Asian form, with forward curved quillons ending in dragon heads. The second is the *pulouar*, which has an Indo-Muslim hilt usually all of steel, with a deep, domed pommel and the same forward curved dragon-ended quillons. Many infantry from the region carried a form of *yataghan* rather than a curved sword. These short swords have straight, single-edged blades with a flat, T-shaped back, and a hilt formed of plates of walrus ivory riveted to the tang, guardless with a hooked pommel. Their scabbards are designed like those of the *shasqa* to enclose part of the hilt. These are called either *salawar yataghan* or *chura* (or by collectors, 'Khyber knife'). A smaller version of the *chura* is used as a dagger and called a *pushqabz* ('hidden hilt'). Though most of these have straight blades, often thinned towards the point to stiletto-like proportions, some have double curved blades. All are usually quite plain.

▶ Sword (*pulouar*) and scabbard

Afghan, 18th century. Purchased 1980 from the Major White collection. XXVIS.180

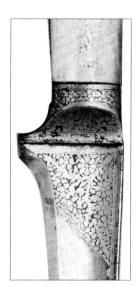

◄ Dagger (*chura*)
and scabbard

Afghan, early 19th century.
Presented by the Indian
Government, 1863.
XXVID.32

Detail of decoration on
the blade.

► Dagger (*pushqabz*)
and scabbard

Afghan, late 18th century.
Presented by the East India
Company 1851. XXVID.78

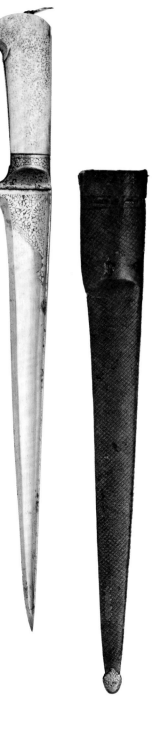

FIREARMS

The popular Afghan form of long gun was a long barrelled matchlock musket with a deeply curved stock, called a *jaza'il*. The matchlock mechanism was introduced by the Turks in the 16th century, and became the standard form throughout India. In the 19th century flintlocks, mostly made in Britain, and percussion locks were fitted to guns of the same type.

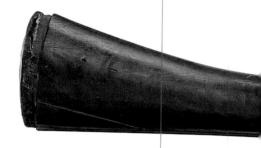

Lock detail

▲ Percussion lock camel gun

Afghan, about 1850.
Purchased 1995. XXVIF.216

SPEARS

▶ Spear (*neza*)

Afghan, early 19th century.
Presented by the East India
Company 1851. XXVII.137

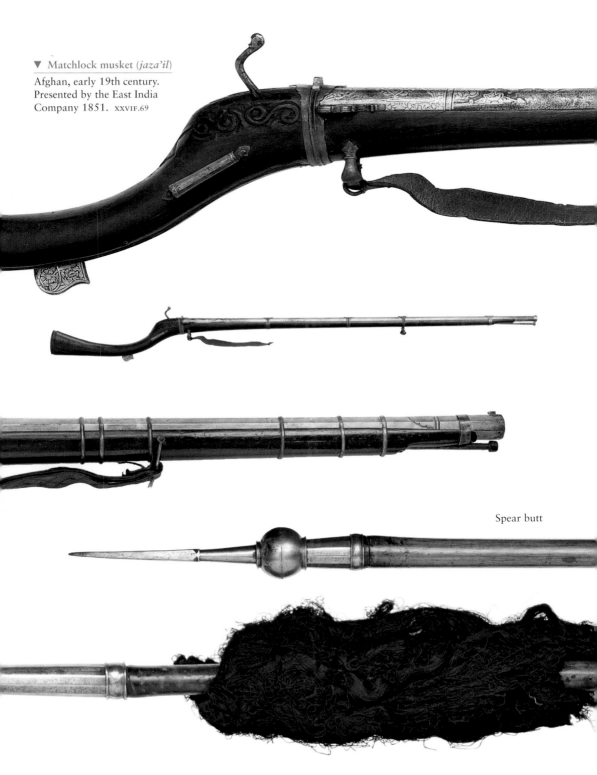

▼ Matchlock musket (*jaza'il*)
Afghan, early 19th century.
Presented by the East India
Company 1851. XXVIF.69

Spear butt

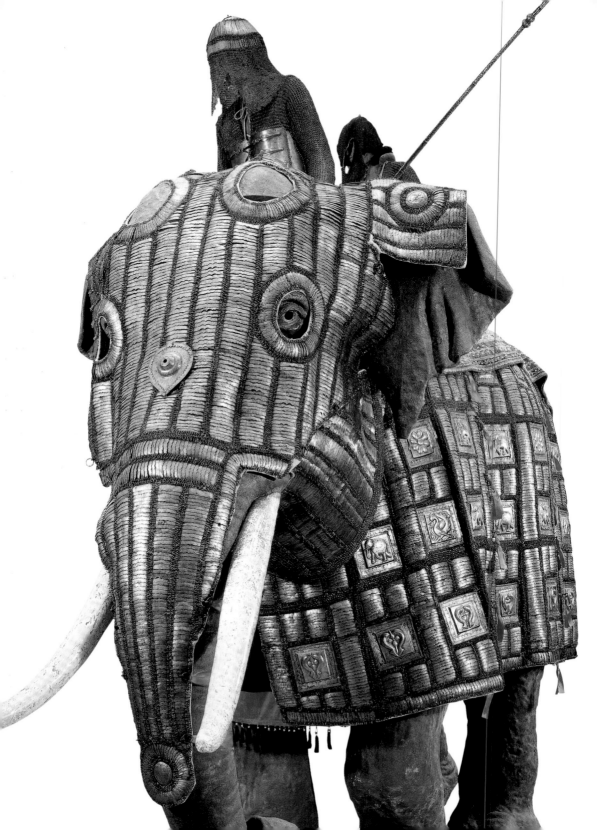

INDIA

The Umayyad conquest incorporated Sindh, at the delta of the Indus, which remained a Muslim province until the 11th century, but it was not until the expansion of the Ghaznavids of Mahmud in the late 10th century that substantial Muslim inroads were made into the north west of India. His son Mas'ud was defeated at Dandanaqan in 1040 by the Seljuq Turks, and re-established the empire in north India in the 11th century. The Ghaznavids were overthrown by the Gurids who captured Ghazni in 1151, and established a slave governor to rule from Delhi. Qutb ud-Din Aibak founded a dynasty called the Mamluk or Slave dynasty, the first of the Delhi Sultanates which expanded their rule to encompass most of the subcontinent by 1350. The Mamluks were overthrown by another group of Turkish *ghilman* cavalry, originally from Afghanistan, the Khalji who had established independent rule in Bengal, and expanded Sultanate rule to the south of India. These in turn were overthrown by the Tughluqs, and the Sultanate reached its greatest extent under Muhammad bin Tughluq. From the late 14th century the Empire of the Slave Kings split into a number of independent sultanates, the main line by the early 16th century being represented by the Lodis.

The founder of the Mughal dynasty, Babur, was a Mongol, descended from Timur (and therefore nominally Genghis Khan, though Timur's descent from the 'World Conqueror' was more for show than fact). Babur established a foothold in India by defeating the Sultanate army of Ibrahim Lodi at the battle of Panipat in 1526, using hand firearms and mobile artillery to defeat the war elephants of the Lodis. Babur was unable to retain his position in India, but his son Humayun re-established control over Delhi in 1555, and Humayun's son Akbar (1556–1605) built an empire which dominated the north of India. The empire reached its greatest extent under Aurangzeb 'Almagir (the 'Earth Shaker' 1658–1707),

◀ Elephant armour (*bargustavan-i-pil*) of mail and plate.
XXVIA.102

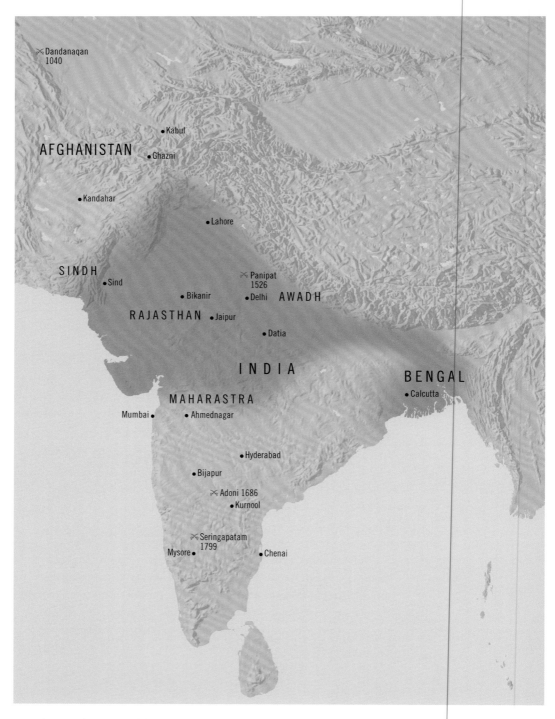

×Dandanaqan
1040

AFGHANISTAN
•Kabul
•Ghazni

•Kandahar

•Lahore

SINDH
•Sind

×Panipat
1526

•Bikanir   •Delhi   AWADH

RAJASTHAN   •Jaipur

•Datia

I N D I A

BENGAL
•Calcutta

MAHARASTRA
Mumbai•   •Ahmednagar

•Hyderabad

•Bijapur

×Adoni 1686
•Kurnool

×Seringapatam
1799
Mysore•   •Chenai

Map showing the extent of the Mughal empire in India under Akbar in 1605.

achieving the same essential extent as the Delhi Sultanate under the Tughluqs, but declined until the last Mughal emperor was deposed by the British for his complicity in the Indian Sepoy Mutiny of 1857.

Though Sunni Muslims, the Mughals were renowned for being tolerant of other religions, as well as being relaxed about the portrayal of the human form and the drinking of wine. With the break-up of the empire in the 18th century, indigenous groups were able to reassert themselves; much of Rajasthan reverted to Hindu dynastic rule, and by the 1760s the Hindu Mahratta Confederation was in control of much of the former Mughal Empire. Only Awadh and Bengal, which asserted their independence under the Muslim Nawabs, Sindh which enjoyed a brief independence under the Baluchi Talpurs, and Mysore, which expanded under Hyder 'Ali and Tipu Sultan remained Islamic, until all were conquered by the British at the end of the 18th and, in the case of Sindh, the middle of the 19th century.

ARMOUR

The armies of the Delhi Sultans and the Mughals reflected their Turkish inheritance. They continued to use light cavalry, but became predominantly a heavy cavalry army composed of Turks, Afghans, Persians, and Hindus. Their principal weapons were the composite bow, sword, and spear. The heavy cavalry wore mail and plate armour (*zereh bagtar*) with helmets (*kolah zereh*), and many of their horses were also protected by armour (*bargustavan*). The armour of mail and plate probably became popular after Timur's invasion of 1398 which reached and looted Delhi. Two styles of mail and plate amour survive from medieval India; a Turkish style, in which columns of small plates are incorporated into the mail at the front and rear of the coat, and a Mughal style, in which the columns of small plates at the front are replaced by one, two or four large plates at either side. The mail of both types is made using a construction common in Europe before the middle of the 14th century, in which alternate rows of links are formed of solid, hammer-welded links and of riveted links. All the known examples of the first type survive from the armoury of Bikanir in Rajasthan where the Rajput client Maharajah Anup Singh deposited the spoils of the siege of Adoni, one of the major cities of the Bijapur Sultanate in the south which he captured for Aurangzeb in 1686. A group of helmets of solid plates, some of them with onion-dome skulls, appear to be from the same provenance, and show considerable similarity to the late 15th-century helmets of the ak-Koyonlu and Timurids. Plate arm defences (*dastana*) accompanied these armours, and the earliest surviving group are characterized by strong points at the elbows. Only one complete example of a Mughal horse armour of mail and plate construction is known to survive, and it is possible that this too came from Bikanir, though its English provenance stretches back into the early 19th century. Likewise only one almost complete elephant armour of mail and plate is known, but the area of India from which it was brought back to Powis Castle in England in the early 19th century is not. Such armours were certainly current in the Mughal armies of the late 16th century, as the *bargustavan* for the horse and the *kajim* or *bargustavan-i-pil* for the elephant are illustrated and detailed in the *'Ain-i Akbari* of Abul Fazl.

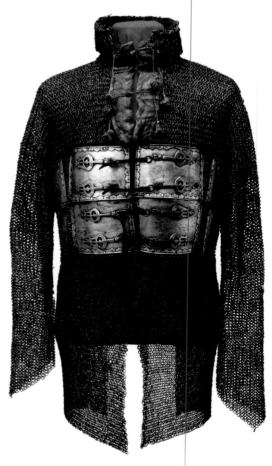

▼ Mail and plate armour (*zereh bagtar*)

Mughal, from Datia, about 1600. XXVIA.148

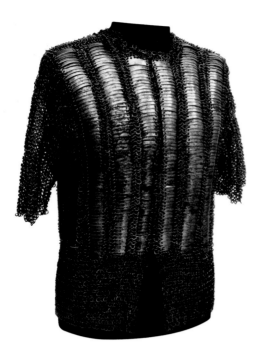

▲ Mail and plate armour (*zereh bagtar*)

Probably Bijapur, 16th century. Purchased 1999. XXVIA.296

From the armoury of Bikanir in Rajasthan, this was captured at the siege of Adoni in the Deccan in 1686.

◄ Elephant armour
(*bargustavan-i-pil*) of
mail and plate

Mughal or Deccani,
probably late 16th
century. Presented in
lieu of death duties,
1962; from the
collection of the earls
of Powis. XXVIA.102

▼ Mail and plate for
man (*zereh bagtar*)
and horse armour
(*bargustavan*)

Mughal, about 1600.
Horse armour
purchased 1832 from
the Bullock Museum
and its successors in
London. XXVIA.203, 258
XXVIH.18

The shield, bowcase, bow,
quiver and arrows are modern
redecorations. The man's
armour is also from Bikanir,
dated 1086 AH (1675/6).

▲ Curved sword (*talwar*)
and scabbard

Mughal, 17th century. AL.290 60

The hilt is decorated in fine gold
koftgari with garden scenes.

The curved cavalry sword was probably introduced into India by the Sultans of Delhi, and by the 16th century had developed a style of its own. The hilt is its most characteristic feature. Often called an 'Indo-Muslim' hilt, it was formed of steel, in one piece with a disc pommel with a central dome for the tang button, and bulbous grip and a pair of short quillons, sometimes with a knuckle bow as well. Such swords were generally called by the Hindi name *talwar*. Some *talwar* had conventional Iranian-style hilts, often decorated with the rich enamels popular in Mughal Successor states such as Awadh and Sindh. The curved talwar spread throughout the Muslim states of India, and very many were found in the armoury of Tipu Sultan of Mysore at Seringapatam after the siege in 1799. The indigenous Hindu sword types also became popular with Muslim cavalry, and many portraits of nobles show them with a *talwar* slung at their side, holding a scabbarded *firanghi*, with a European broadsword blade and a Hindu basket hilt, in their hands.

▲ Curved sword (*shamshir*) and scabbard

Sindh, probably early 19th century. XXVIS.7

This sword has a watered steel blade and enamel decoration on the hilt, the pommel of which is carved as a ram's head. Swords of this type were characteristic of the taste of the Talpur rulers of Sindh.

Maker's signature.

▲ *Kard*

Central Indian, dated
1122 AH (1710/11).
Purchased 1990.
XXVID.143

Made by Muhammad
Baqir, with a stained
ivory hilt.

▲ Dagger (*khanjar*)
and scabbard

Mughal, about 1650.
Purchased 1990.
XXVID.144

Rock crystal hilt set
with rubies.

▲ Dagger (*khanjar*)
and scabbard

Mughal, late 17th
century. Purchased
1990. XXVID.145

Serpentine hilt carved
in the form of a
horse's head.

INDONESIA

▼ Map of South
East Asia.

Muslim traders were regular visitors to the south east Asian states from the 7th century; sites such as Siraf on the Persian Gulf attest to the volume of sea-borne trade between Persia and China from the Tang dynasty onwards. The earliest Muslim ruler was a Hindu rajah of Kedah in peninsular Malaysia, who converted to Islam in the 12th century. The tiny Sultanate of Ternate in the Moluccas (Maluku Islands) was established in the late 13th century, and the major Hindu Sultanate of Malacca, ruling much of Malaysia and Sumatra, converted to Islam early in the 15th century, and the Sultanate of Aceh remained Muslim after the Portuguese overtook Malacca in the 16th century.

A member of the Javanese Majapahit royal family at Demak converted to Islam late in the 15th century, starting the growth of Islam on Java, and marriage into the ruling family of Bantam led to the creation of a Muslim Sultanate there, ruling south Sumatra and west Java. Indonesia rapidly became a battleground for European colonial powers, and Islam became by the mid 20th century a rallying call against colonial rule. After independence in 1945, some 88 per cent of the population were Muslim.

DAGGERS

The characteristic edged weapon of Indonesia is the *kris* (or *keris*), usually regarded as a dagger, sometimes the length of a short sword. Adult males all wore a *kris* outdoors, usually tucked into the sash at the back. The *kris* has a double-edged blade, usually wavy, sometimes straight, widening asymmetrically at the hilt, where the lower edge flares off to a point and the upper is carved with notches (*grenang*). This upper section of the blade is called the *ganja*. Its unusual form can be traced back to the Majapahit period in the 14th century, and some scholars suggest that it can be traced back to the 11th century, or even to Chinese dagger-axe blades (*ge*) of the Warring States period which have been excavated in Indonesia and which exhibit a very similar asymmetrical form. The blades are pattern welded, forged of different steels, traditionally including meteoric iron, which when etched produce a dramatic dark and bright wavy pattern (*pamor*). A pistol grip hilt, carved of wood, bone or other material, is glued to the tang, with a decorative ferrule or *mendaq* between the two. Most *kris* hilts are of angled pistol grip form, usually richly carved. One of the most elegant forms has the pommel in the form of a kingfisher; this type was made in Malaysia. The scabbard (*sarong*) is of wood, carved with a broad boat-shaped section at the throat (*wrangka*), the length often covered with brass sheet (*pendoq*). *Kris* blades were kept as heirlooms for many generations, and often fitted with hilts and scabbards of different regional styles. Some straight, slender bladed *kris* were used for executions in parts of Indonesia; the blade of the *kris* was pressed through the victim's back, piercing his heart.

▼ Sword (*Kris*)
Indonesian, Lombok, 19th century. Presented by Colonel Sanders. XXVIS.285

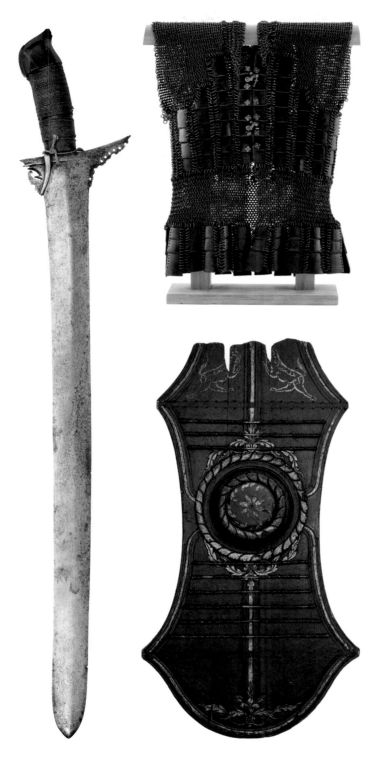

◀ Mail and plate armour of horn

Philippine, Moro, 19th century. Old Tower Collection. XXVIA.69

SWORD

◀ Sword (*Kris*)

Far left: Philippine, Moro, 19th century. Old Tower Collection. XXVID.162

SHIELD

◀ Shield (*klau*)

Philippine, Moro, 19th century. Old Tower Collection. XXVIA.172

GLOSSARY

abu fitila	Matchlock musket (Arabia)
affedali	Snaphance lock musket (Morocco)
akinjis	Light cavalry (Turkey)
allarh	Spear (Tuareg)
altit	Snaphance lock musket (Morocco)
'amud	Mace (Persia)
arnautka	Miquelet lock musket (Bosnia)
assagai	Spear (Berber)
at alinlici	Shaffron (horse's head defence) (Turkey)
ayar	Shield (Tuareg)
az-zaghayah	Spear (Berber)
baasoo	Spear (Sudan)
bargustavan	Horse armour (India)
bargustavan -i-pil	Elephant armour (India)
bazuband	Arm defence (Persia)
budiak	Spear (Philippines)
çakmakli tufek	Miquelet lock musket (Turkey)
çekiç	War hammer (Turkey)
çelina	Pistol (Bosnia)
chahar a'ineh	Cuirass (Persia)
chahar kham	Composite bow (India)
chura	Knife (Afghanistan)
çiçak	Helmet (Turkey)
çubuklija	Miquelet lock musket (Bosnia)
dastana	Arm defence (India)
dhal	Shield (India)
dir'	Mail armour (Arabia)
dizçek	Thigh defence (Turkey)
dzerferdar	Miquelet lock musket (Herzegovina)
eyer	Saddle (Turkey)
firanghi	Sword (India)
fitilli tufek	Matchlock musket (Turkey)
flyssa	Knife (Kabyle)
fursan	Heavy cavalry (Persia)
ganja	Upper section of a *kris* blade (Indonesia)
gardani	neck defence for a horse (crinet) (Persia)
ge	Dagger axe (China)
ghulam	Slave soldier, pl. ghilman (Turkey)
giddamiyah	Dagger (Arabia)
golok	Knife (Malaysia)
gorz	Mace (Persia)
grenang	Notched section of a *kris* blade (Indonesia)
hancer	Dagger (Turkey)
janbiyya	Dagger (Arabia)
janissaries	Infantry corps (Turkey)
jarid	Javelin (Persia)
jawshan	Lamellar coat (Persia)
jaza'il	Matchlock musket (Afghanistan)
jibbah	Quilted coat (Sudan)
jund	Army (Persia)
Kabyle	Berber people, also a snaphance lock musket
kajim	body armour for an animal (horse or elephant) including peytral, flanchard and crupper) (Persian, Indian)
kalkan	Shield (Turkey)
kaman	Composite bow (Turkey, Persia, India)
kampilan	Sword (Philippine)
kard	Knife (Persia, India)
kariophili	Miquelet lock musket (Greece)
karkal	Brigandine armour (Turkey)
kasan	Ear of a composite bow (Turkey)
kaskara	Sword (Sudan)
katar	Dagger (India)
kattara	Sword (Arabia)
khanjar	Dagger (Arabia, Persia, India)
khepesh	Sickle sword (Egypt)
kiliç	Sword (Turkey)
kindjal	Dagger (Caucasus)
klewang	Machete (Sumatra)
koftgari	Gold decoration, 'false damascening' (India)
kolah khod	Plate helmet (Persia)
kolah zereh	Mail and plate helmet (India)
kopis	Sword (ancient Macedonia)
koummya	Dagger (Morocco)
kris	Dagger (Indonesia)
kubur	Pistol (Turkey)
kuburluk	Pistol holster (Turkey)
kudi	Machete (Java)

kujang	Machete (Java)		*saq*	Leg defences (Persia)
ledenica	Pistol (Montenegro)		*separ*	Shield (India)
lembing	Spear (Malaysia)		*shamshir*	Sword (Persia)
loi-bo	Arm knife (Sudan)		*shasqa*	Sword (Caucasus)
machaira	Sword (ancient Macedonia)		*shast*	Thumb ring (Persia, India)
mandau	Machete (Borneo)		*shishane*	Miquelet lock musket (Turkey, Persia)
mendaq	Fitting between blade and hilt of a *kris* (Indonesia)		*shotel*	Sickle sword (Ethiopia)
migfer	Helmet (Turkey)		*sipahis*	Heavy cavalry (Turkey)
misiourka	Helmet (Caucasus)		*siyah*	Ear of a composite bow (Arabia)
mukhala	Miquelet lock musket (Morocco)		*tabarzin*	Saddle axe (Arabia, Persia, India)
neza	Spear (India)		*tajfaf*	Horse armour (Persia)
nimcha	Sword (Morocco)		*takouba*	Sword (Sudan)
pajama zireh	armoured trousers (India, Persia)		*talwar*	Sword (India)
pamor	Pattern on a kris blade		*tamgha*	Tribal symbol (Turkey)
paragun	Miquelet lock musket (Bosnia)		*tançika*	Miquelet lock musket (Bosnia, Albania)
parang	Machete (Malaysia)		*taouzilt*	Snaphance lock musket (Morocco)
parang ilang	Machete (Borneo)		*telek*	Dagger (Sudan)
pazipent	Arm defence (Turkey)		*tombak*	Gilt bronze (Turkey)
pendoq	Brass cover of a *kris* scabbard (Indonesia)		*tombak*	Spear (Java)
pulouar	Sword (Afghanistan)		*toradar*	Matchlock musket (India)
pushqabz	Dagger (Afghanistan, India)		*turs*	Shield (Persia)
qama	Dagger (Caucasus)		*wrangka*	Boat-shaped section at the throat of a *kris* scabbard (Indonesia)
qashqah	Head defence for a horse (shaffron) (Persia)		*yataghan*	Knife (Turkey)
rasak	Miquelet lock musket (Serbia, Croatia)		*yelman*	False edge of a kiliç (Turkey)
rencong	Dagger (Sumatra)		*zereh bagtar*	Mail and plate armour (India)
rijjala	Infantry (Persia)		*zirh*	Mail shirt (Arabia)
rumh	Lance (Arabia)		*zirh gomlek*	Mail and plate armour (Turkey)
saif	Sword (Arabia)		*zirh gomlek gobekligi*	Mail and plate armour (Turkey)
salawar yataghan	Knife (Afghan)		*zlatka*	Pistol (Balkans)

FURTHER READING

Alexander, D 1992 *The arts of war: arms and armour of the 7th to 19th centuries. The Nasser D. Khalili Collection of Islamic Art.* London, Nour Foundation (UK) Limited in association with Azimuth Editions and Oxford University Press

Astvatsaturyan, E G 2002 *Turetskoe oruzhie (Turkish weapons).* St Petersburg, St Petersburg, Atlant

Astvatsaturyan, E G 2004 *Oruzhie narodov Kavkaza (Caucasian weapons).* St Petersburg, [publisher unknown]

Egerton of Tatton, W 1880 *An illustrated handbook of Indian arms*. London, W H Allen (2nd edition of 1895 includes an appendix on Egerton's own collection, bequeathed in 1910 to the Manchester City Art Gallery, reprinted Bangkok, White Orchid Press, 1981)

Elgood, R (ed.) 1979 *Islamic arms and armour*. London, Scolar Press

Elgood, R 1994 *The arms and armour of Arabia in the 18th, 19th and 20th centuries*. Aldershot, Scolar Press

Elgood, R 1995 *Firearms of the Islamic world in the Tareq Rajab Museum, Kuwait*. London, I.B. Taurus

Elgood, R 2004 *Hindu arms and ritual: Arms and armour from India, 1400–1865*. Delft, Eburon Academic Publishers

Elgood, R 2009 *The arms of Greece and her Balkan neighbours in the Ottoman period*. London, Thames and Hudson

Grayson, C E, M French, M J O'Brien 2007 *Traditional archery from six continents, the Charles E Grayson Collection*. Columbia, University of Missouri Press

Hales, R 2013 *Islamic and Oriental arms and armour: a lifetime's passion*. Robert Hales C.I. Ltd

Karpowicz, A 2008 *Ottoman Turkish bows, manufacture and design*. Sackville [publisher unknown]

Mohamed, B 2008 *The arts of the Muslim knight: The Furusiyya Art Foundation Collection*. Milan, Skira Editore

Rawson, P S 1968 *The Indian sword*. London, Herbert Jenkins

Richardson, T 2007 *An introduction to Indian arms and armour*. Leeds, Royal Armouries

Ricketts, H and Missillier, P 1988 *Splendeur des armes orientales*. Paris, Acte-Expo

Robinson, H R 1967 *Oriental Armour*. London, Herbert Jenkins Ltd

Stone, G C 1934 *A glossary of the construction, decoration and use of arms and armor in all countries and in all times*. (Facsimile reprint. Mineola, New York, Dover Publications, 1999)

Tirri, A C 2003 *Islamic weapons, Maghrib to Moghul*. Sarasota, Indigo Publishing

Zonneveld, A G van 2001 *Traditional weapons of the Indonesian archipelago*. Leiden, C. Zwartenkot Art Books

The right of Thom Richardson to be identified as the author of this work has been asserted in accordance with the Copyright Designs and Patents Act 1988.

Series Editor: Debbie Wurr
Series Designer: Geraldine Mead
Series Photographers: Gary Ombler, Rod Joyce

Base maps: Mountain High Maps™ Copyright ©1995 Digital Wisdom, Inc.

Royal Armouries Museum, Armouries Drive, Leeds LS10 1LT

© 2015 The Trustees of the Armouries

ISBN 978-0-948092-71-8

Printed by W&G Baird

Every effort has been made to trace the copyright holders of the images used and we apologise for any unintentional omissions. We would be pleased to insert the appropriate acknowledgment in any subsequent edition of this publication.